Working the Streets

A handbook for Christians involved in outreach to prostitutes

Ruth Robb
and
Marion Carson

NCAP

Produced by The National Christian Alliance on Prostitution
Door of Hope, 22a Hanbury Street, London E1 6QR

Published by New Wine Press, PO Box 17, Chichester PO20 6RY,
United Kingdom

ISBN 1-903725-19-4

Typeset by CRB Associates, Reepham, Norfolk
Printed in England by Bookcraft

Dedication

To Helen who died,
who made reaching out
an encounter with God's heart
for the lost and the found.

*'I am not ashamed of the gospel
because it is the power of God for
the salvation of everyone who believes.'*

(Romans 1:16)

Contents

NCAP

The National Christian Alliance on Prostitution
exists to unite, equip and empower groups
working with people involved in the sex industry
to offer freedom and change.

Acknowledgements

Many people have contributed to the production of this manual. In particular, we want to thank:

- **Mark** and **Sarah Perriot**, who passionately believed that what had been learned by experience should be written down. Sarah spent many hours writing dictated notes.

- **Rachel Jamieson**, **Jo Wakeling** and **Morag Gunn** for their insights into working the streets in London and Glasgow.

- **Dr Fiona Merriweather** for her professional knowledge on the health problems of sex workers.

- **Laurence Singlehurst**, who encouraged us to finish this book!

- **Penny Weightman** for proof-reading the final text

In addition, the support of **Jonathan Edwards** for the initial graphic design work involved has been very much appreciated.

A real answer to prayer has been Clive Birks of CRB Associates and Ed Harding of New Wine Press. They became involved in perfect timing and often we thank God for their spiritual integrity and professional expertise. Without their generosity this manual would not be in print.

An acknowledgement would never be complete without mentioning fellow NCAP trustees: Theresa Cumbers, Mark and Jo Wakeling, Di Martin, Clair Gorman, Pam Hand and Paul Lapsley, who have been the 'Aarons' and 'Hurs' of this ministry.

In closing, we acknowledge the support of our husbands – Douglas Carson and Ken Robb – who have listened!

Foreword

This manual represents much of the love, experience and understanding that the authors and other Christian workers have spent in seeking to help the women on the streets of the United Kingdom – seeking to demonstrate the love of God and help them. Not only to consider an alternative life off the streets, but also, and perhaps controversially, to know how to protect themselves and keep themselves from dying if they remain on the streets.

I commend this manual to you because I know the people who have written it care desperately and have put many hours and much of their lives into caring for women on the street and seeking to love them for who they are.

You will find the information in this manual invaluable. Essential reading for any church or agency who is seeking to reach out to women who have been caught up in prostitution of one sort or another.

Laurence

Laurence Singlehurst
Director, YWAM England

Introduction

This manual contains information gathered through ministering to working girls in Soho, Earl's Court and King's Cross in London, and also in Glasgow. Its aim is to equip those who want to take the love of God to those who are caught in the web of prostitution. We believe that this can be done through the power of the Holy Spirit and by showing the gentleness of Jesus to the women as we get alongside them and build relationships with them.

The first part of this book will give basic information about the prostitution scene, how to set up an outreach, and how to minister to and disciple the girls. The second part will deal with practical matters in greater detail, in some cases giving particular pointers for ministry within the specific area of need. An appendix gives some information on drugs and their effects.

It would be wrong to generalise and say that the behaviours described in this book are those of all prostitutes. It is important to remember that behaviour patterns and working practices vary in individuals, cities and cultures. For example, in some cities girls tend to have pimps, and in others they are more likely to work independently. Nevertheless, there are similarities, and we hope that the information given here will be beneficial for outreach workers wherever they work. Our experience has been gained in the UK, but we hope that those working in other nations will be able to benefit from what is written here, and adapt it according to the cultural setting in which outreach is taking place.

The sex industry in the UK and throughout the world is huge, and much of it goes on in massage parlours and escort agencies. Due to the secrecy which inevitably surrounds this area it is virtually impossible to reach out to the girls involved in this kind of work. This book must therefore be limited to street-working and the problems which occur for those involved in this way of life, simply because this is where the expertise and experience lies. Please do make it a matter of prayer that somehow God will enable us to reach the many girls who are caught up in the kind of prostitution which is less visible and may even have a veneer of respectability and glamour.

This guide is intended primarily as a resource, but also as a stimulus to further discussion and study. Throughout the book we have made statements about certain issues, such as abortion and testing for human immunodeficiency virus (HIV), with which you may not agree. We hope that the opinions expressed here will be the basis for group discussion within the team, at training sessions or in a college setting. The longer you work with the women, the more questions you will undoubtedly have. Reading widely on a subject gives you different perspectives on your own experiences as well as giving you further practical information for your work. In addition, reading about others' experiences and learning about similar ministries to your own will greatly encourage you as well as teach you. We have provided a list of books which we have found to be particularly useful, and which we recommend for further reading.

For those readers who are new to, or unfamiliar with, this kind of ministry, the very nature of the material of this book means that you will be reading things you may not be accustomed to thinking about. This means that you may find some of the topics and language offensive. You may be shocked – but you will be shocked on the streets. You may find that it raises areas of vulnerability, weakness or sin in your own life. If you find that this happens, these areas need to be talked through and prayed through with another mature Christian. Please do pray before and after studying this book, and don't underestimate the spiritual battle involved in this kind of work. Remember that the foundation for every area of our lives as believers is the Word of God itself, and that everything we do must be for God's glory.

'Finally, brothers, whatever is true, whatever is noble, whatever is right, whatever is pure, whatever is lovely, whatever is admirable – if anything is excellent or praiseworthy – think about such things.' (Philippians 4:8)

PART 1

CHAPTER 1

Prostitutes and those who reach out to them

*'He will respond to the plea of the desitute;
   he will not despise their plea.'*

(Psalm 102:17)

1.1   Prostitution in context

Prostitution is the practice of selling sex. A client or 'punter' pays for sexual favours from a woman, or less commonly, a man. Prostitutes may work alone in some cities, have 'pimps' in others, or work in brothels or massage parlours. The common factor is that they receive money for providing sexual services. In the UK it is illegal to solicit publicly; to live off the immoral earnings of another person; and to run a brothel.

There are many reasons for prostitution. Some prostitutes go 'on the game' to pay for a drug habit, others to supplement benefits or wages. Still others make prostitution their full-time job. Differing theories exist as to why women become sex workers. For example, many sociologists would say that women become prostitutes because of poverty, while some psycho-analytic theorists would argue that a sexual 'neurosis' or dysfunction (such as being over-sexed) is the cause. From the point of view of Christian outreach, it is simplistic to give only one reason for the phenomenon of prostitution since experience tells us that each woman has her own needs and circumstances which are often very complex. While there is undoubt-edly a place for research into the causes of prostitution, our task is to learn to see each girl as an individual, as a precious creation of God, made in His image. As far as our outreach to individual women is concerned, we will stress in Chapter 4 that knowledge of all the facts about an individual's background should not be necessary – God calls us to love unconditionally.

Some women enter prostitution voluntarily, seeing it as a way to earn money. For example, a young girl, perhaps still at school, might see prostitution as a way to supplement her family's income or to provide herself with money. Others may feel that they have been forced into prostitution by circumstances, eg a drug habit or extreme debt; or if they feel they cannot support their family on their existing income. Some are forced into the sex industry by other people. For example, young girls may be 'groomed' for prostitution by older boyfriends who later turn out to be pimps. In the UK, children may be forced into selling themselves, and then have to give the money they earn to an adult. This kind of behaviour does go on, but it is far more common in countries in the Far East. For example, there is a huge trade in young girls between Thailand and its neighbouring countries. Uneducated girls from poor backgrounds are brought into Thailand, and charged a fee for their passage and board. They are then shut up in brothels, often in cramped, isolated and unsanitary conditions. The money they earn from their customers is then taken by the brothel owner to repay the debt the girl has supposedly incurred for her passage and board. Often this charge has been extortionate, and there is little chance of the girl ever paying off the debt.

The situation is usually rather less dramatic in the UK, but it is important to realise that sex slavery does exist even here. Recently, the press has been highlighting a trade in women who have sought asylum from countries such as Albania and the Baltic states. They come to the UK to seek work and become trapped in the sex industry in major cities such as London and Manchester. It has also been reported that some illegal immigrant women are brought into the UK specifically for the purposes of prostitution. Perhaps the most common way, however, is for those girls who are already working on the streets to have 'pimps' who take the money the girls earn and insist that they go out to work, often beating them up if they try to protest. If they try to escape they are usually found again, and their lives may be at risk.

1.2   Secular attitudes to prostitution

Many people work with prostitutes in an attempt to help the girls improve their lives. Health professionals, for example, will provide needle exchanges, condoms, and regular health checks. Social workers may try to help with housing problems and family difficulties such as child care. In many cities, health and social workers have collaborated to operate drop-in centres in which needle exchange and clinics are available. Girls can also go to these places to receive advice.

Secular agencies may have varying attitudes towards the sex industry. For some secular outreach workers, prostitution is the archetype of female exploitation, the prime example of the subjection of women to men, and an indication that society is fundamentally sexist, male-dominated and oppressive to women. This view entails the idea that prostitution is unnatural and that no woman would want to sell herself for sex unless she had to. Those who espouse this view are likely to think that prostitution in and of itself is wrong, and that it should be stopped, or at least controlled in some way.

For others, notably some feminist thinkers (although not all feminists take this view), prostitution is a legitimate way for a woman to earn a living. A woman should have the right to decide what she does with her body, and if she sells herself for sex she is earning her living as legitimately as any woman in a standard job such as secretarial work or teaching. Indeed, some would say that a woman who takes charge of her body in this way and is her own boss (in effect she is a business woman) is more free than those who are under contract to an employer. Those who take this view tend to think that prostitution should be legalised and that health facilities should be available to sex workers as their right. They see outreach not as a way of helping a woman to change her lifestyle, but as a way of empowering her to earn a living in the way she has chosen. It is argued that prostitutes should be able to form associations and trade unions like any other group of workers, that they should have the right to lobby members of parliament, and that the sex industry should be made legal.

Although feminist thinking is becoming increasingly influential in policy decision-making in the UK, most secular agencies do not take the view that women should be empowered to earn money as they please. While these agencies do not include God in their thinking, their standpoint tends to be the same as that of Christian agencies – that we should try to help women to leave prostitution and to achieve their full potential in other, more fulfilling ways. There is a general recognition among health and social workers that a prostitute's lifestyle is harmful and that damage limitation is required in areas in which prostitution takes place. In other words, there is a recognition that prostitution carries inherent health risks, most notably through infection, and that if good care and advice can be provided, not only will the girls' health be likely to improve but also the health of the general public can also be kept at a reasonable standard.

In the early part of the 20th century, and indeed the early days of outreach to prostitutes, the main criterion for intervention was the limitation of sexual infection. In particular, during the Second World War, there was concern that public health was at great risk if servicemen became infected by prostitutes and through promiscuity in general. There was a feeling that prostitutes were the main source of venereal disease, the incidence of which did indeed soar during the war.

Today, the rationale is somewhat different, as far as health is concerned. Venereal disease is still a problem – gonorrhoea and other infections are still around. But the advent of widely-available antibiotics has rendered this previously chronic problem more easily solved. Today the health risks surrounding prostitution are largely connected with HIV and acquired immune deficiency syndrome (AIDS). This is why health boards provide on-the-spot needle exchanges and issue condoms as well as health advice and primary treatment.

1.3   Christian outreach

As Christians our view of prostitution is primarily dependent on the view taken in the Bible. There are several main points we wish to highlight here.

- The biblical view is that sexual activity should be confined to marriage. This is God's intended best way for His people.

- The Old Testament law does not approve of prostitution – any woman who 'plays the harlot' becomes unclean, and, if she is the daughter of a priest, she should be put to death by burning (Leviticus 21:9). The law is also insistent that 'immoral earnings' should not be used in the Lord's work (Deuteronomy 23:18). Prostitution is something which is undesirable, both from the male point of view and from the point of view of the woman herself. In Amos 7:17, the prophet is told that, as a punishment for Amaziah's hostility towards Amos, Amaziah's wife is condemned to a life of prostitution. The implication seems to be that prostitution is not a good life for a woman; it is a poor way to live, and the person condemned to this life is to be pitied rather than condemned for what she does. It may not be her fault but her husband's that this fate should befall her.

- The Bible also uses prostitution as a metaphor for faithlessness among God's people, Israel – those who are unfaithful to God are described as 'playing the harlot', ie as having other lovers than God Himself (Hosea 4:12; Isaiah 23:16).

- The Old Testament therefore recognises that prostitution and general lawlessness tend to go hand-in-hand. For this reason prostitution should be curtailed as far as possible. However, the idea that it should be eliminated completely does not seem to be tackled as a viable possibility. The Old Testament recognises that there is a social stigma attached to prostitution, and certainly says that prostitutes are somehow unclean (Jeremiah 3:1–3). But it also recognises that not all women take on the role of harlot voluntarily. For this, compassion is in order, as is a recognition of the fault of men for imposing prostitution on some women.

- In the story of the spies to Judah, we are told that Rahab, who helps the spies by hiding them, is a harlot. This fact, however, is not dwelt upon in the story. Rather, the writer depicts her as one who knows who God is and declares this, and is shown as someone who is concerned for her family's safety. She can be used by God in His plans for His people, just as any other woman can be. The New Testament writer to the Hebrews states that she did what she did by faith in God: despite the fact that she is a prostitute she too can live and act by faith and be commended as such. She is never condemned for being a prostitute: God's grace prevails.

- In 1 Corinthians 6:15–16, the congregation in Corinth is warned that it should not go to prostitutes for sexual favours, because the Corinthian Christians are to be distinctive as a separate community. Once again, prostitution is accepted as a matter of everyday living, but as something towards which believers should have a distinctive attitude – men should not use prostitutes. It is remarkable, however, that in the gospels, the prostitute is not openly condemned for her harlotry but commended for her ability (above others) to believe the message and enter the kingdom of heaven (Matthew 21:32). Indeed, Rahab the harlot is cited as one of Jesus' ancestors (Matthew 1:5). Once again, grace is the key to our understanding of why we should love and not condemn sex workers.

- Therefore, rather than go out with the attitude that what they are doing is wrong, we should be seeing prostitutes as people made in God's image, whom Jesus loves and longs that they would have a relationship with Him. Jesus Himself had a reputation for mixing with people who were beyond the social pale, accepting them as they were, but yet urging them to 'go and sin no more'. It is certainly true, as we have seen, that the Bible does not approve of prostitution, but it also recognises that these women are individuals who can be used by God. They are not worthless people, but of infinite worth in His sight.

1.4   Reasons for being there

Many of the women you serve will have become separated from their families. They may have left home because of a breakdown in relationships with their parents or guardians. They may have left home willingly or have been rejected by the family and thrown out.

There may be many reasons for this. Many prostitutes have been sexually abused by a parent or relative. There may have been violence within the home, with threats and fighting being a way of life. Others may have been rejected by their parents because of drug abuse, alcoholism or repeated involvement in crime. Others may have become homeless following the death of their parents, or the arrival of a new step-parent. Some women may have been brought up in children's homes and moved into hostels during their adolescence.

Fragmented families can produce fragmented people. If a woman comes from a broken home or has been rejected by her family, her pain will be great, even after many years of separation. For some, even the distorted world of prostitution can provide a sense of belonging for those who feel that they do not have any roots. Isolation in the home can produce people who are attracted to other isolated people, eg other sex workers, addicts, or vagrants. They may experience a temporary or spasmodic sense of belonging, but the pain of separation from families will never fully go away.

Case study

Prostitutes and those who reach out to them

Heather worked the streets in King's Cross and Earl's Court in London. She was an active lesbian, dealt in cocaine, and was the pimp of two women. One night she was beaten up and had to have 16 stitches to her head as a result of wrong dealings with drugs and conning a punter. The next night, when she met the outreach worker on the streets, she asked for prayer and felt the power of the Holy Spirit. Her addiction to drugs disappeared and she was filled with joy. Her chaotic lifestyle stopped. She began to pray constantly and became a special blessing to everyone whose life she touched.

Two years after her 'Damascus Road' experience, Heather was murdered by one of her ex-pimps. He could not bear to see her so happy. He killed her to stop the joy that he wanted but knew he couldn't have unless he changed. He went to prison for eight years, and would not allow anyone to visit him.

Ruth writes:

Heather grasped grace, and knew she was equal to anyone because of Jesus. I was deeply affected by her death, and, ten years later, I still cry when I think of her murder. It seemed so senseless. I cried out to God and remembered Enoch in Genesis 5:24:

'Enoch walked with God, then he was no more, because God took him away.'

Heather had not been afraid of her ex-pimp, but she always knew it was a possibility that he would try to kill her. He had threatened her constantly. I felt that God had said 'enough is enough' and took her away from all the memory of the suffering in her life into a place in which there is no past, but only the present – with Jesus.

CHAPTER 2

Street working and prostitution

'It will happen that in the very place
where it was said to them,
''You are not my people,''
they will be called ''sons of the living God''.'

(Romans 9:26)

2.1   The prostitution 'scene'

As we have said, prostitution is not limited to city streets. There are many more women who work in escort agencies or massage parlours. Some work from their own homes, having built a clientele of regular customers through advertising in telephone boxes, magazines, and shop windows, and through agents who frequent clubs and public toilets in railway and underground stations. Here, however, we are concerned with the women who are visible on inner-city streets. As you learn more about prostitution, and become more familiar with life on the streets, always remember – 'there but for the grace of God go I.' You too could have made wrong choices in your life or had unavoidable circumstances which led you into a life different from the one you know.

The area in which prostitutes work is often known as their 'beat'. Some areas of a city may be very busy for two to three years, and then the women may move to a new area. The change in venue could be owing to police harassment, or the protests of residents and local business people such as shopkeepers. It might also be owing to in-fighting among the workers themselves or among their pimps. If drugs are involved, it may be necessary to change district in order to avoid police raids or even raids on the part of other pimps and dealers. Sometimes pimps and ponces move women to other areas on a regular basis in order to prevent them from forming relationships with anyone other than their 'manager' himself.

So-called red-light districts are often situated in tourist areas where there are hotels, railway and bus stations, harbours and docks. Prostitution, however, is not limited to the rundown areas of cities and towns. Women are to be found in high-class residential areas where the respectability provides a façade that hides what is really happening. By the same token, not all women dress up in stereotypical stiletto heels and fishnet stockings. Often they work in jeans and trainers.

As far as the clients (or punters) themselves are concerned, the quieter the area the better, because this reduces their chances of being recognised as they try to pick up a woman. If a beat becomes congested, pimps and independent working women tend to move on to other areas. In very large and busy neighbourhoods, violence tends to erupt because of increased competition among workers; this will be greatly increased if drugs are involved.

The constant change of working areas can be very frustrating for agencies which are trying to reach the women. However, the very presence of these agencies may contribute to the move. For example, clinics and drop-in centres, however well-disguised, draw attention to the fact that prostitution is taking place in the area. Furthermore, agencies which bring the power of prayer into any area will certainly contribute to the fluidity as people's lives become affected and they are changed into the people God intends them to be. Women who are against such change will probably move away to find a place in which they feel more comfortable.

2.2 Prostitution and the law in the UK

A brothel is a place to which people go for the purpose of illicit sexual intercourse. According to Scottish and English law, a flat or house from which a woman works alone does not constitute a brothel. Accordingly, some women, once they have built up a clientele, may find they no longer need to go out on the streets.

As far as street-working is concerned, kerb-crawling (or soliciting a woman for the purposes of prostitution) is illegal in England and Wales, and currently carries the penalty of a fine. There is no law against kerb-crawling in Scotland, although the common law offence of breach of the peace can be applied. It is, however, relatively easy for a man to pick up a woman in a red-light district. On the whole, police try to limit prostitution to specific areas in cities, so that some degree of surveillance and control may be maintained.

2.3 Rent boys

Throughout this guide we refer to women prostitutes as the main people with whom you will work on outreach. However, it is possible for men to be prostitutes too. Often, these men are known as rent boys. Rent boys may be bisexual (ie attracted to either sex), homosexual, or heterosexual in orientation, and may even have children. Many rent boys are motivated mainly by the need for money to sustain their lifestyle or their drug habit, or to support their children. Rent boys tend to work solo. They are generally between 14 and 40 years of age.

Some male prostitutes who are homosexuals may also work as transvestites, ie dressed in women's clothing. They usually perform oral sex for clients, who may not realise that the prostitute is a man. Other punters may deliberately seek out a transvestite prostitute.

Some punters prefer male transsexual prostitutes (men who have had an operation to become female). For example, a married man who feels guilty about having homosexual desires may try to ease his conscience by having sex with a transsexual. For such clients, transsexuals are an 'acquired taste' and are sought after on the beat. On the other hand, the client may also regard the transsexual as weak. In our experience, more than any other working group, transsexuals are frequently victims of verbal, sexual and physical abuse from their clients, other transsexuals, and drug pushers.

For some male transsexuals, working as a prostitute fulfils the need to be recognised as a woman. It is quite usual for a transsexual to work with a female prostitute. They work in the same way as female prostitutes, picking men up on the streets. On the streets, transsexuals are commonly known as 'trannies'. They can be easily identified as they tend to exaggerate their feminine qualities, for example, they may adopt a swaggering walk and feminine hand movements.

2.4   Pimps

A pimp, ponce, or manager is someone who forces one or more women to work for him. The women give their earnings to their pimp, who regards himself as providing a service to the punters. Ex-working women have been known to manage other prostitutes when they are too old or worn out to work themselves.

Ponces often move workers around so that they cannot form relationships or bonds with other prostitutes. Some may insist that women work in one city during the week, and in another at weekends. It is essential for the ponce to make the woman feel that she is dependent on him and to be completely loyal to him. He will provide her with money, and drugs if she needs them. Sometimes, a regular customer (perhaps motivated by guilt) may want to help the woman get away from street culture. If this comes to the ponce's attention, the woman can be moved on. Similarly, if there is a help agency in the area, the pimp may move the woman away. Pimps want to exercise control over every aspect of the women's lives – it is a kind of latter-day slavery. Pimps are often quite sexually confused – they may well be bisexual. They may have a drug habit to maintain and also be drug suppliers. Their lives can be as miserable and enslaved as those of the women they control.

Most women desire to be in relationship with men and to be one with them in a healthy way (Genesis 3:16). Those who become prostitutes do not stop having those needs. As one woman said, 'Even prostitutes need love and need to be needed and wanted by a man.' However, the lifestyle of a prostitute brings about distorted perceptions as to how such needs may be met, and some women may find themselves trying to fulfil these needs through misplaced loyalty to a ponce or even a punter, however ruthlessly they may be treated by them. Some women have never experienced non-destructive relationships and therefore have no idea as to what might be 'normal'. The emotional and spiritual consequences of being a prostitute make it hard for them to choose what is right because their sense of integrity has been eroded. Standards of right and wrong may change depending on whom they are with. However, for some, a degree of the 'love deficit' might be fulfilled in their work because they feel needed by the punters and believe that they make them happy. They may also have a sense of being taken care of, and of having decisions made in their interest, by their ponce, who is strong, protective and always there.

Some women may appear not to have a ponce and to be working independently. However, most likely there is a man at home waiting for the woman's earnings. Working women may not talk about their ponces, partly because they are afraid of them, and partly because they want to appear to have the dignity of independence. It is quite common for a woman to feel ashamed, to pretend that she works independently and to deny that she is under the control of a ponce. She may feel ashamed that she is under the control of another person and be afraid of being told that she should have known better.

2.5 Clippers

A clipper is a male or female prostitute who takes money from clients without providing the sexual services promised. Most clippers start out as prostitutes, but have changed 'career' because of bad experiences while they were working. For example, they may have been raped, stabbed or robbed. For those who are ill (for example, those who have AIDS or cancer), it is less exhausting than working.

Clippers enjoy the excitement of what they do since it is like gambling – taking risks makes them feel more adequate, and give them an adrenaline-high to which it is easy to become addicted. Clippers work in groups and can be very protective towards each other. They tend to work in tourist areas where there is easy prey. Clipping is more risky since the penalty for theft is generally more severe (perhaps 18 months in prison) than it is for soliciting, which may be only a fine. Police tend to raid clipping areas more frequently and vigorously than a normal working beat. Clippers are also more likely to be assaulted than their counterparts in prostitution.

2.6 The work

How do women pick up their clients? They will approach the client (or the client will approach them) and ask, 'Do you want business?' A price and service is agreed; the worker and client may go off together immediately or they may arrange to meet in ten minutes in one of a number of venues, eg a hotel, the client's own accommodation, an alleyway, or the woman's own house (where her children may be present). Usually, women work in pairs and discuss their clients with one another.

It is rare for a girl to be asked for 'straight' sex (ie heterosexual intercourse). The following requests are common:

- group sex with two or more clients and two or more girls
- lesbian sex watched by the client
- oral sex
- masochistic sex (eg whipping)

- anal sex

- 'talking dirty'

- observation of girl masturbating

- masturbation of client

- 'counselling' – the client may just want to talk

2.7 The mindset of survival

Prostitutes constantly work in a potentially dangerous environment. They are at risk of attack from their clients, and possibly also from their pimps. As a result they have highly-developed observation skills and can assess a character very quickly. They assess the client's cleanliness and demeanour; is he looking scared or threatening? Does he look naive? Is he alone? (Prostitutes are very wary of men in groups.) The first approach to the client – in which the girl asks, 'Do you want business?' – is the most honest part of the relationship between the girl and the punter. The rest is based on a fantasy of human sexual fulfilment.

Prostitutes try to set themselves standards or principles. For example, they may vow never to go with a client who does not pay the full fee at the beginning. They may say that they will not go in a car which is dirty, or refuse to perform certain sex acts which they detest. Some women state that they do not go with men from different ethnic backgrounds to themselves. However, real life often means that these principles have to be set aside, for example, if the woman needs money for drugs, to give to her pimp, or to pay bills.

Prostitutes become very adept at talking their way out of emergency situations. For example, the client may produce a knife and threaten an individual worker. Or a punter might refuse to let the worker go, or demand more than was originally agreed. The client may be testing the prostitute to see if she becomes afraid, and he may gain some pleasure from her fear. The worker may take the pressure out of the situation by doing what is asked, without showing any emotion, particularly fear, and maintaining friendly verbal communication.[1] It is possible in this type of situation for the client to gain pleasure from the fact that the woman does not show any fear. Sometimes, however, this strategy does not work, and the girl may be raped, robbed, or stabbed. Rape is considered to have occurred when the punter does not adhere to the original agreement which was made when the punter picked up the prostitute.

---

[1] Unfortunately, this method of survival may become habitual. The woman may use it to deal with any problem. She may honestly believe that if she talks through a problem, the problem is eliminated and no practical steps need be taken to change or help herself and her circumstances. To help women recover from a prostitution lifestyle, it is crucial to help them appreciate that choices must be made and actions taken, with no gap between what is said and what is done.

Most workers carry knives or tools with short blades for self-defence. Sometimes the knife may be used to demand more payment than the client originally agreed. Clients may be assaulted, or even find themselves ambushed, attacked and robbed. Assaults of this kind are seldom reported to the police because the victim may be too embarrassed to admit that he was looking for a prostitute.

Workers build up regular client lists and may go to the client's home. In these situations the woman may feel that the punter is her friend and the relationship changes. This friendship could last many years, and its possible termination can be a source of great fear for the worker. However, there is sometimes an expectation that it will end as sharply and coldly as it began.

For many sex workers, genuine love is the goal which they use to justify their existence, and they dream that one day they will find it. Films which glamourise prostitution, such as *Pretty Woman*, fuel this dream.

We all search to find our identity. Believers find their identity in Christ and in Him alone. However, among such a suppressed people group, real identity is scarcely known. Few people know who they really are, and they seek their identity in the wrong places. Pray that we may help girls to be brought out of introspection and into the knowledge of Jesus. In other words, pray that they will be able to look away from themselves and be able to see Jesus, who longs to lead us to the Great Shepherd and protect us so that no-one can snatch us from the Father's hand (John 10:30). Above all our prayer must be that girls would be committed to Jesus and find who they really are. Jesus longs to set them free so that they can become who God intends them to be. Our mandate is to help them discover a personal relationship with Him, so that they may change from the inside. We do not focus on behaviour, or the fact that they are prostitutes, but on the fact that they are loved by Him.

2.8 Reasons for being there

Many prostitutes have spent time in various institutions: children's homes, approved boarding schools, rehabilitation centres, prisons, hospitals and hostels. For many people with this background, life can become a reaction against their institutionalised past. They live for freedom from rules and regulations. Ironically, their very search for freedom leads them into another set of rules, the rules of the streets, where the enforcer is the pimp, the drug or the compulsion to work.

Institutions take care and responsibility out of the community and place it in the professional sphere. They also segregate people from mainstream society. People may be institutionalised because something has happened to them (eg abuse in the home), because their environment has been unsuitable (eg neglect or homelessness), or because of something they have done (eg crime).

Institutions can rob a person of individuality. Many workers who have been through institutions are very unsure of their identity, since they have not been treated as individuals with individual needs. If they have never felt that they are special in the eyes of another person, they will certainly not realise that they are special in the sight of God. As a result they become like their present peer group. For example, while on the streets, they will adopt the language and behaviour of those around them. It is also quite possible for new believers to adopt Christian jargon very quickly in an effort to fit in more easily.

A person who has been institutionalised finds it very hard to follow self-imposed guidelines and keep a daily routine. Some girls who have spent many years in institutions may even wish to return to one for a short time, as life becomes more and more out of control on the streets. For example, as things become more complex for a worker – drugs, working, violence, debt and warrants – she may realise that to go to prison for a short time will give her some form of relief, because she cannot gain control of her own life. Unfortunately, many who have been institutionalised are very likely to return to the old way of life as soon as they leave prison.

Case study

The people who make the scene

Sandra described herself as a 'hopeless slag'. For one of her punters, who liked to be called Uncle Jimmy, Sandra had to dress up as a schoolgirl, and play the part of a submissive niece.

Sandra found this very difficult because she had a real Uncle Jimmy, who had bought her presents and given her lots of attention while at the same time abusing her sexually from when she was nine years old until she was 14. This new Uncle Jimmy paid her very well – enough to buy two days' supply of heroin. For Sandra, however, this meant that once more she felt like a ping-pong ball, her drugs and punters such as Uncle Jimmy controlling her life.

She came to church a few times, and thoroughly enjoyed singing and reading the Bible. Sandra's favourite verse was Psalm 27:4:

> 'One thing I ask of the LORD,
>   this is what I seek:
> that I may dwell in the house of the LORD
>   all the days of my life,
> to gaze upon the beauty of the LORD.'

However, although she was a mother, Sandra had never really matured emotionally. She remained a little girl who needed someone to tell her what to do, and she never really realised the seriousness of what she was doing with drugs. She died at 25 of a drug overdose.

CHAPTER 3

Starting a ministry – building a team

'It does not, therefore, depend on man's desire or
effort, but on God's mercy.'

(Romans 9:16)

In this chapter we will offer pointers for starting your ministry. We will outline some important procedures and policies which, if set up at the beginning, will help you to cope with the various situations which will arise as you reach out to the women. For example, we will consider recruitment, confidentiality and some aspects of good team management, and strategies for ensuring that your work has the spiritual support it will need.

In Chapter 4 we give more detailed guidelines on the practicalities of outreach itself.

3.1   A note on motives

When you go on outreach, remember why you are there. You are there because you believe that Jesus has asked you to go. You are there because you have been commanded to love God with all your heart and soul and strength, and to love your neighbour as yourself. It is a matter of obedience. What is your first priority? You may say that you are there to bring people to Christ. This, of course, is a reasonable enough response. However, at the risk of shocking you, we would like to say that this should not be your main reason for going on outreach. If you go out with the idea that you are going to lead people into conversion, you are running the risk of becoming a scalp hunter, someone who wants a conversion for his or her own satisfaction. This will happen if you focus on salvation rather than people. Always remember why Jesus was sent by God – it was because God loves the world. Jesus' priority was the people: He loved them first, and that was why He went among them. When He was accused of being a drunkard and a glutton, we do not hear that He necessarily changed these people (on the contrary the business of changing was very much seen as the individual's responsibility), merely that He spent time with them. He was known for being the friend of people whom most of society rejected. Why was He there? Because He knew that these people were the beloved creatures of God. Yes, He wanted them to be in a restored relationship with God, but He was there in the first place because He loved them.

This, too, should be your motivation. Anything other than this will prevent you from building a true relationship with prostitutes. If a woman feels that you are targeting her for any reason other than love for her, she is very unlikely to respond to you. If, on the other hand, she sees that you do love her, she is more likely to begin to trust you. If you go out with the intention to convert, rather than to love the women, you will find it all the more difficult to cope if the women continuously reject your attempts to lead them to Christ. So, before you go out, make sure your motives are pure. Is it a case of conditional love – that if they do not do what you want them to do, you will eventually reject them? Or will you, like Christ Himself, continue to love the woman for herself even though she does not turn to the Lord?

This kind of attitude should also help you to avoid feeling that you are going in to 'rescue fallen women'. If you are thinking that prostitution is a wrong which you want to help eradicate, two things will probably result. First, you will meet with discouragement early on. As we saw in Chapter 1, prostitution has always been around and it probably always will be. You are not going to change things. Second, you will most likely go out with a judging attitude which the women will surely pick up on. They will inevitably detect that you are more concerned with what they do than with who they are. Once again we say that this will only hinder you from building relationships and introducing individuals to a personal relationship with Jesus.

3.2   Preparing the ground

Your priorities at the beginning are prayer (a prayer walk around the area is a useful thing to do) and getting to know the streets. Get a map of the area you intend to work in and familiarise yourself with all the streets. It is also useful to know its history – has prostitution always happened there? Is there a history of violence? This kind of information will help you to build up a feel for the area and the spiritual forces which are at work in it.

- Introduce yourselves to churches in the local area and gain their prayer support for your work.

- Each team member should have an identity card, with his or her photograph on it, along with the address of your team base.

- Introduce yourselves to the local police and vice squad. Get the police to stamp the back of your identity card.

- Research local resources for the women so that you will be able to have an effective referral system, eg housing, health clinics, legal advice, Department of Social Security (DSS), and so on.

- Have a written statement of purpose to which all members of the team subscribe. This will help the team to be focused in its work.

3.3   Getting started

Prayerfully decide on your method of outreach. Some groups may want to take tea, coffee or soup with them as they go on outreach, and use this as a basis for getting to know the people on the beat. Others work on the principle that relationships and the fact that you are there are more important. You will also have to decide whether or not you will take condoms to give to the women. Some people do this on the premise of damage limitation, ie to help prevent the spread of HIV and other sexually transmitted diseases. Others feel that statutory agencies already provide this service and that to hand out condoms is an implicit encouragement for the women to continue as prostitutes. These are matters for which it is best to pray about as a team, and do what you believe God is telling you.

At first there may only be two of you who wish to start an outreach ministry. However, to make your outreach consistent you will need to take on others to help you cover holidays and times when team members are unwell. As you build up your team, we recommend that you interview prospective outreach workers, using believers, whom you know and respect, as the interviewers. It is useful to have a team of two or three experienced interviewers. Make the interview semi-formal, doing as much as you can to make the candidate feel at ease. We suggest that each candidate provides two references, one of which should be from their church pastor or elder. The work you are recruiting for is important and the women deserve the respect of a team which has gone through a reasonable selection procedure.

Many women have become prostitutes as a result of their treatment by men – for example, some are forced into prostitution by boyfriends. Others may have had a bad relationship with an abusive male partner or have come from families in which they have been abused. On the beat there is often a tangible anti-male sentiment, and a subconscious or conscious desire to have their revenge on men. It can be very healing for the women to have a man as part of the team, showing them that there are men who can be compassionate and caring and live within proper boundaries. Male team members must be prepared to be rejected at first because the women will associate them with violent experiences, and they should always work in partnership with a female member of the team. It is also good to have a man on the outreach team for safety reasons.

3.4 Tips for good team management

Ensure that the gifts of the team are used. Don't expect everyone to have the same talents and skills. Many are called to work with prostitutes, but some may not be called to go out on to the streets. Someone who is gifted in fund-raising may not be gifted in evangelism, or someone who is an intercessor may not be good at liaising with other agencies. In other words, don't try to strait-jacket the calling of an individual – allow them to be obedient to what God has called them to do.

Once the gifts have been identified, establish boundaries. Someone should be designated team leader, and each member of the team should be sure of his or her job description and role in the team. This will help to avoid confusion and conflict.

Devise good communication strategies: outreach rotas and regular meetings help to make sure everyone knows what is going on in the team. Outreach is a team exercise: tell your colleagues what is happening and pray together about the women you meet. Have debriefing sessions in which you share traumatic stories and incidents with each other.

Devise a system of written notes and information. As and when you talk with a woman, write a brief note of what happened. It is good, when you first get to know a woman and become involved in her care, to ask her to fill in a background information form (giving her address, date of birth and other personal details). All these documents are confidential (see below) but are available for other team members to consult if they need to. It is not always possible for the same team member to be around when a girl needs someone. This kind of communication promotes continuity of care, and also helps prevent ministry to any particular woman becoming centred exclusively around one team member. There is, however, no need to pressurise women for information (address, date of birth and so on); it will be revealed in the natural course of the relationship.

Make sure each member of the team has a support group of at least two people who will meet to pray for her own personal and spiritual needs. These should be people who are spiritually mature and whom you respect, who will tell you the truth and guide you, warning you against making mistakes and helping to pick you up when you do, or when things become discouraging (as they most certainly will!). Prayer is a responsibility, and this mechanism should help ensure that it is carried out. There is great power in agreement in prayer.

Always tell your support group exactly when you are out so that they can pray for you. If you tell them about any of the women, use false names. Remember, too, to communicate with your prayer chain. It is sometimes a good idea to ask the women's permission before you tell the prayer chain: this is good way of reminding them that what you have is different from the service of social workers, nurses and so on. Problems which may be relayed to prayer chains as a matter of urgency include homelessness, arrest, a diagnosis of HIV, or if someone receives Jesus. Use the faith of your prayer support.

Find older believers and Christian leaders whom you respect and establish a council of reference or advisory board, so that if you find yourself in any difficulties as a group, you can get some good pastoral advice. The advisory board can also give you advice on fund-raising, supervise individuals and help evaluate the performance of the team. They can be asked to review, monitor or assess a specific programme of action which you are proposing.

Have a fund-raiser, someone who is gifted in persuading people both to give money and to do things to raise it, as well as being able to liaise with grant-giving organisations.

3.5   Confidentiality

It is essential that you have a confidentiality policy. It is very much a part of your ministry to be able to keep confidences. Only in this way will women be able to trust you and build a relationship with you. It is crucial that a woman knows that whatever she says to you will not be repeated to other people. Confidentiality extends to other outreach workers, other women, and other volunteers. Here are some basic guidelines:

- Have a locked cupboard in which to keep notes and records, and make sure you do use it. In general, if a woman asks to see her notes, she has a right to do so. This does not apply, however, to letters sent to you from medical practitioners; these are strictly confidential and you should ask permission of the doctor before anyone outside the team sees it.

- If a woman asks you if you are able to keep confidential something she is going to tell you, explain first of all that it depends on what she is going to say. There may be occasions when it is necessary to share something with another team member in order to get some advice on how to handle a situation. Or, if you are involved in a social work case conference or court case you may find that you are under pressure and must disclose information about a woman. In such cases you might ask permission of the girl to share it with someone. False names are useful in prayer chains and prayer letters.

If you think it necessary to break a confidence, it is useful to ask yourself the following questions:

- Does it benefit the worker if another professional body knows this information?

- Will the woman perceive it as beneficial if another professional body has access to this information?

- Is breaking the confidence here bringing glory to God or bringing light into the situation?

- Am I keeping silent because I am afraid that the worker will reject me?

- Are my feelings and affections stronger than my principles of right or wrong?

- Am I disclosing information in order to look good in other people's eyes?

- Am I talking because I need to, for my own well-being? If so, to whom am I speaking?

- Am I just enjoying a gossip?

Secrets, darkness, and fear of disclosure are Satan's way of operating. The truth is revealed in order to set people free. Sometimes, we set rules for ourselves which are intended for our guidance. However, these can sometimes become replacements for the unique guidance of the Holy Spirit. It is good to have rules, particularly in areas such as confidentiality. They set down the baseline of what is acceptable and what is not. However, it is important that rules don't become strait-jackets; remember the letter of the law kills but the Spirit gives life (2 Corinthians 3:6). Each individual is unique, and is loved by Christ as unique – take the wise counsel of older, more mature leaders if necessary, and don't allow rules to stifle the Spirit.

3.6   Spiritual health checks

Maintain your own spiritual health. It is important to understand at the outset that believers who enter a ministry to prostitutes are entering into an area in which the forces of darkness are given the upper hand by those who live and work within it. The spiritual battle which this type of work involves should not be underestimated. Addiction, promiscuity and general lawlessness among men and women are the very areas of life which open up a way for Satan to work. Because of this, we cannot stress enough the importance of maintaining your own spiritual health, through worship, prayer and Bible study, both privately and with other believers. We recommend that each member of the team has a personal support group, to whom they are accountable in prayer, and who keep what is said in strict confidence.

We cannot emphasise enough the importance of prayer in the life of the team. You are entering into areas of the world in which the powers of darkness have been allowed to exercise control. It is crucial to ensure that a mechanism of prayer is in place for the work of the team as a whole, but it is also crucial for your own spiritual well-being that your set up a system whereby you are accountable to others for your own relationship with God. You are doing work which the powers of darkness do not want to be done. They will do everything they can to hinder you from bringing light into the dark areas. Make sure you stay close to the source of light, constantly keeping Jesus at the centre, so that it can shine through you.

Establish a prayer chain for the work of the team. It also helps to produce a newsletter fairly regularly to keep all members of the team informed of developments within the work, and about each other, as well as giving information about the sex industry in your urban area.

'Do not be anxious about anything, but in everything, by prayer and petition, with thanksgiving, present your requests to God. And the peace of God, which transcends all understanding, will guard your hearts and minds in Christ Jesus.'   (Philippians 4:6–7)

Meet together as a team regularly for worship. In order to learn to minister in His power at all times, worship must be the foundation of the work. In Acts 16:19–26, we read that during their imprisonment, Paul and Silas, who had been beaten with rods and attacked by the crowd, were worshipping God at midnight. As they were praying and singing hymns, God opened the prison doors and loosened their chains – all through worship.

3.7 Some things 'to be'

- **Be patient.** Sometimes God might require you to pray in, and for, an area for some months before you meet a prostitute. This is so that you can come to understand the specific spiritual strongholds, curses, and spiritual history and why it is a working area. It brings power and effectiveness into the ministry to have these answers before beginning outreach.

- **Be realistic.** Have a realistic idea of what you are getting into. You will be enthusiastic at first, but this might wear off, especially if the weather is bad! Perseverance is required in all aspects of the Christian life and particularly in mission work of this sort in which you may not always see the fruits of your labour. Make long-term, as well as short-term, plans and goals which will keep your vision alive.

- **Be open.** Build up relationships with other agencies and groups working in the area, both statutory and voluntary. In the UK there is certainly a bias against Christian organisations among the social services – but don't allow this to make you attempt to hide your motivations and working practices. Be light in the darkness in this respect, too. Work alongside and liaise with other Christian groups. Let them know you are there and what you are doing.

- **Be yourself!** There are many statutory and voluntary bodies which will be doing essentially the same work as you – building up relationships, being concerned about health and housing, writing court reports and generally trying to help the girls improve their quality of life. You want to be different – you want to bring the light and love of Christ into their lives.

'You are the light of the world. A city on a hill cannot be hidden. Neither do people light a lamp and put it under a bowl. Instead they put it on its stand, and it gives light to everyone in the house. In the same way, let your light shine before men, that they may see your good deeds and praise your Father in heaven.'   (Matthew 5:14–16)

Case study

Separation from children

While many women will have left their families, still others will have had their own children taken away from them. In many cases, this will be because their chaotic lifestyle means that they are unable to look after their children. Their children may have been taken into care by the social work department, or be looked after by other members of their families. Some women will have had children whom they have never known because their babies were adopted at birth. Others will be living with the pain and anguish of having had abortions.

Whatever the situation, if a woman's children have been taken into care or are being looked after by another member of her family, she will most probably want to get them back. She will probably feel the separation very keenly. The return of children can be a very powerful incentive for a woman who is going through rehabilitation.

CHAPTER 4

Outreach:
steps in building
relationships

'The Spirit of the Sovereign Lord is on me,
because the Lord has anointed me
to preach good news to the poor.
He has sent me to bind up the broken-hearted,
to proclaim freedom for the captives
and release from darkness for the prisoners.'

(Isaiah 61:1)

In this chapter we will take you through the process of outreach and discipleship – from the initial preparations which have to be made each time you actually go out on the streets, to the time when you help a girl to be integrated into a church. We fully acknowledge that every area and situation is different, but we hope that the guidelines given here will help you to build a ministry which is appropriate to your area and the people with whom, and for whom, you work, and that they will help you to cope with the inevitable pitfalls which will occur as you carry out your calling.

4.1   Going out on the streets

- Find out when the beat is busiest. Be prepared to be flexible in your timing as necessary.

- Before going on outreach, pray together as a team.

- Remember, always work in pairs, never go out on your own.

- Carry a small NIV Bible with you on outreach; underline verses and passages you believe are appropriate for ministry. You are obeying God's command to be in the world, serving His people, and following Christ's example to be among the poor. You have the weapons which Christ has given you – use them:

  'For though we live in the world, we do not wage war as the world does. The weapons we fight with are not the weapons of the world. On the contrary, they have divine power to demolish strongholds.'

  (2 Corinthians 10:3–4)

- Have a stock of cards which have Scripture verses or prayers on them. The women appreciate them.

- Carry your identity card (which includes a photograph) at all times.

- Keep warm. Outreach at night can become very cold. Wear several layers of clothing and watertight boots or shoes. Remember too that clothes and make-up can be a common interest between the women on your team and those whom you meet on the streets – something to talk about and enjoy together.

- Use a small notebook to keep notes and information; write down any special incidents which take place while you are with the girls.

- Arrange to meet other members of the team at regular intervals while you are out on outreach. Always know where other team members are.

- Don't expect to get up at 7 am if you have been out on the beat until 4 am!

If you find that you do not enjoy outreach, that you dread going out every week, think about your motives. Are you in the right place? Should you be serving in some other aspect of the ministry, such as in the prayer team or support group? God wants us to enjoy our ministry, and if you are not comfortable and fulfilled by it you should perhaps be serving in another way. The women are very astute and will detect that you are miserable and wishing you were not there!

4.2   Meeting the women

When you first make contact with sex workers on the streets, it is imperative that you communicate that you are Christians and say why you are there. Don't use this as an opportunity to witness: they will see through this straight away. Only talk about the Lord if they are interested. It is important that they see that you love them as people and not just as someone to be converted and 'improved'. You are not setting out to notch up another conversion on a 'salvation score card'. At first, be content with perhaps only saying hello. Do hand out relevant information as to where the team can be contacted.

Remember that first impressions are important – and lasting – and that the women have, by necessity, learned to sum up people very quickly. They can soon tell if someone is being judgmental towards them or not being straight with them.

Also remember that in new areas of outreach, relationships can take a long time to be established. You will need to have patience and realistic expectations of what can be achieved. The women will have experienced a lot of rejection in the past and may well have rejected themselves. Don't expect them to accept you immediately. If you are consistent in your outreach, ie keeping regular times and consistently being there when you say you will, this will be much more effective than if you are irregular and only go out when you feel like it. For example, going out once a week on the same day is more effective than going out twice in one week and not going out at all the next week.

Don't expect instant results. Evangelism, just like discipling, is a process. It may be some time between your initial meeting with the woman and telling her about Jesus and her turning to Him (if at all). And always remember that while you may not see the results of your sowing, God works in ways that we don't understand. You may find results you could never have imagined.

Rather than responding to needs – listen to God. There will be many crises, and it will not always be appropriate or necessary for you to act immediately or even become involved. Continuous prayer is the key to knowing where and when to do things.

Be imaginative in your outreach. For example, distribute flowers and Easter eggs at Easter.

Have an appointment system with the women as part of your outreach, for example meeting Samantha at 1 am in Burger King, Gill at 2 pm in McDonalds, Helen at 3 pm at the station, and so on.

4.3   Prioritising needs

On outreach it is essential that your work be spiritually led, not needs led. There are countless organisations in this country which cater for the women's physical, financial and social needs. You are different! You are bringing light into a dark area – something that no government agency or non-Christian charity can do. Of course this does not mean that you will not deal with the physical and financial problems, but it does mean that you have an extra dimension – the spiritual, the presence of Christ. So, once you have made it clear as to what you are about, if the woman is still interested, arrange to meet her outside outreach time, with another team member.

As you meet the women, you will find different responses. Some will be more than willing to talk to you, others will hang back, others may even be hostile towards you (possibly because they are more interested in making money than in talking to you!). Some will immediately tell you their life stories, while others will tell you of their problems, eg with housing, their children and so on. A good idea is to offer to pray with and for these women who are so open with you. If you have a prayer chain in operation you can offer to put their prayer concern onto it, with the full assurance that it will be confidential to the prayer chain and will go no further. Most women will recognise Christ in you and have some sense that there is a mighty God who can change their lives. They will probably be touched by your offer of prayer. When women are hostile it does not mean that they do not see Christ in you, but that they do! They may feel their lifestyles or even their very selves (ie their identities) are threatened by the goodness of Jesus.

Knowing the facts about a woman's background can help us to understand why she has gone into prostitution, and we may think that this will help us to be compassionate in our dealings with her. In many cases, it may be difficult to get to the reality of the situation, which may even be unclear in the woman's own mind. She may see only injustice against her and give partial or even untrue versions of her story. It is not necessary to find out the whole story of her past. Christ compels us to love unconditionally, and only He knows everything about each one of us, including those things of which we may be ashamed or which are too painful for us to talk about.

Always remember, every woman you meet is made in the image of God. Sometimes the image is distorted and broken, but God has called us to touch people as He does – with unconditional love and to touch and bind up the broken-hearted, just as He does. It is imperative that this is our starting point and continued focus when reaching out to the women.

4.4   Follow-up

Now that you have met the women, there will be some whom you feel it is appropriate to meet again, outside their working environment. As you gain experience you will become able to discern those who have a real interest in your message, those for whom you are simply another 'social service' and those who just want a listening ear. Whatever the case, you have an ideal opportunity to share the love of Jesus, and a chance to build relationships which will bear fruit for Him.

- Always consult a colleague and pray with them before you commit yourself to an individual woman. There is tremendous power in agreement in prayer.

- If possible, try to meet the woman in her home or somewhere which is neutral territory. This may be a café, Burger King or McDonald's. This will increase the woman's feeling of security and enable her to speak more freely with you.

- Before the meeting, arrange with your outreach partner who is going to deal with the physical and social problems and who is to be the spiritual mentor. Establishing roles and sticking to the agreement like this is essential – the woman you are working with needs to know the boundaries of the relationship; that way she will feel more secure. At the meeting, the practical issues of her life can be addressed, eg the date of her last health check, how her children are, housing problems, and so on. This is an ideal time to offer to pray again and to speak words of God's love for her into her life.

- Make sure you turn up for the meeting – but don't be surprised if she does not. Remember these women have chaotic lifestyles, and that another meeting can be arranged. Take relationships slowly, responding to the woman's heart, not her urgent needs.

- When you are counselling a woman, don't start with the fact that prostitution is wrong. Similarly, don't start by aggressively telling her the gospel. This will only alienate her, making her feel that you are only interested in what she does rather than who she is. Rather, start with the obvious 'painkillers' she is using in her life, eg drugs, alcohol, relationships or other addictions. These are the things she probably most wants to change, and she will be more pre-occupied with these, and how she can get help, rather than how she can stop working.

- Allow one-and-a-half hours for the initial interview. The top priority for you is to explain exactly who you are, communicating your salvation without preaching and always focusing on Jesus as the answer to her needs.

■ Assess the practical issues. For example, she may need a house or to undergo detoxification, be worried about debt, and so on. State clearly which realistic goals can be reached and in what timescale. Issues which may be covered are:

Family:	Isolation, rejection, children
Drugs:	Overwhelming habits, different methods of stabilising, methadone treatment, cold turkey and prayer
Rehabilitation:	Giving pre-rehab counselling and making applications to rehab units and clinics
DSS:	Sorting through or commencing claims
Legal matters:	Outstanding court cases or warrants
Housing:	Seeking permanent accommodation
Health issues:	Drug-related problems such as abscesses, HIV/AIDS
Working:	Are they practising safe sex? Do they have present fears about the dangers of working, eg assaults on women or murders?
Discipleship:	This is the most important. Jesus acted and then spoke to a now receptive audience. Let's spur each other on to a balance of works, wonders and words.

■ It is useful to have a small card with emergency numbers, such as the emergency social work service, hospitals, rehabilitation units, housing officers, and so on. Include on this list the contact number for the base or group from which you are working. If you are aiming to help with any pressing problem such as health or housing, try to articulate accurately what realistic goals can be achieved and in what timescale.

■ Be trustworthy. Carry out any actions you agree to take on her behalf.

■ Many women have a multitude of problems to overcome. Remember that in God's eyes, however, there are no problems, only opportunities! This is where your prayer partner comes in. Seek God's agenda for the area which should be brought to light first. Remember, too, that God's agenda may not be the same as yours, or what you might expect, so be careful and don't try to manipulate either the woman or God.

■ There is no formula for putting needs in order of priority, only the working of the still small voice of God.

4.5   Moving into discipleship

As you meet with individual women regularly, you will get to know them, their likes and dislikes, and their habits. It is at this point that the real need for perseverance becomes obvious. Sometimes you will feel that you should give up, that there is no point in continuing to meet with a woman. You will experience disappointment as some let you down, some perhaps become ill, or disappear from the scene. You may have to 'forgive seventy times seven' or recognise that someone you are working with no longer wants your help, and have to let go. The more experience you have, the more you will be able to gauge situations. As you lean on God you will learn what the priorities of your own ministry should be.

- Listen carefully to what the woman has to say. Often you will hear half-truths, or exaggerations. 'White lies' are common, the real truth being undermined or glossed over. This may be acceptable in everyday society, but it is not acceptable to God. Aim for reality. You will learn by experience to recognise white lies and half-truths; learn, too, to put new confidence in God each day. He is the best teacher.

- Many workers adopt different personas to help them survive their chaotic lifestyles. They find they need to wear different masks in different situations. For example, a worker may have taken different names for when she is at work and when she is at home, or when she has to appear at court. Indeed, it is possible for a woman to adopt so many personas that she forgets who she was originally. In Old Testament Hebrew thought, the name signifies the personality – who that person is (eg Saul changed his named to Paul to signify the complete change of his identity in Christ; God, on the other hand, remains the great I AM). Thus, when a woman begins to adopt different personas by taking on different names there is a real risk of her identity and personality becoming disintegrated.[1]

  The habits and attitudes which are the result of this kind of behaviour can take years to unlearn as the person becomes whole in Jesus Christ. When the dysfunction is as profound as this, words are not very powerful and actions of love are required. Jesus performed miracles first and spoke later. Actions produce a trust relationship between the woman and the one helping her. In all her confusion she needs to see the person of Jesus and not simply hear words spoken.

  'For the kingdom of God is not a matter of talk but of power.'
  (1 Corinthians 4:20)

When you pray for her, always ask for wisdom as to how to intercede for her.

  'Surely you desire truth in the inner parts;
  you teach me wisdom in the inmost place.'   (Psalm 51:6)

---

[1] There is a condition known as multiple personality disorder. It is very rare and requires very skilful and specialised treatment. It is quite different from the conscious adopting of different personas which is a symptom of mental 'ill-health' and is described here. If you become involved with someone who has 'multiple personalities', you should seek specialist psychiatric advice, and follow it!

■ Invite the woman to come to church with you, or perhaps take her to an Alpha course. Above all, be consistent in your behaviour. Meet regularly with her for counselling. Or if you can't make it, arrange for someone else to take her to church, and so on. If, and when, the woman has a clear understanding of who Jesus is and who she is in Jesus, then counselling can begin to tackle any addiction problems she may have. Each counselling session should be set up to deal with a specific issue. That is, it should be a disciplined session – the conversation and prayer should address specific issues and not be allowed to ramble or get out of control. Ask God to show you why this problem is surfacing, ie look for the root causes. When you meet her, stick to the agreed agenda! If it is appropriate, discipling can be continued alongside counselling, but still with clear boundaries in place, ie the woman should be quite clear about which member of the team deals with practical issues, who the counsellor is, and that discipling takes place through the church. At an appropriate stage, the woman can be encouraged to go to a housegroup or other small-group setting within the church.

■ Ask the Lord to protect you and your families against the specific spirits which are operating in the person you are praying for. Be diligent in your own walk with Jesus.

> 'Put on the full armour of God so that you can take your stand against the devil's schemes. For our struggle is not against flesh and blood, but against the rulers, against the authorities, against the powers of this dark world and against the spiritual forces of evil in the heavenly realms.'
>
> (Ephesians 6:11–12)

Domestic violence

Many sex workers have been victims of, or witnesses to, domestic violence. This need not simply be physical abuse within the home, but may also be emotional or sexual abuse. Some women may have been raped by their husband or partner. Other women will have witnessed violence toward their mother by their father. As you get to know a woman, you may begin to suspect that she is being abused at home. Here are some guidelines for dealing with this situation.

■ If you suspect that a woman is being abused, it's wise not to ask her directly, as she may feel that she is being coerced into talking when she does not wish to. It can be helpful to ask a general question such as, 'Are you having problems at home?'

■ Document what she tells you and record how she is – her appearance and her emotional state. Remember that this may be used in court if she decides to take legal action. Your testimony may help her later. Write down her own words, eg 'My boyfriend tried to strangle me,' rather than your own impressions.

- Know the address and staff of your local women's refuge. Don't try to be the expert, but be aware of those who are, and work alongside them.

- Check if it is okay to contact her at home; if not, arrange an alternative method of meeting or contact.

- Be aware how difficult it is for women to leave an abusive partner. Some women may leave many times before they leave permanently.

- However, it may be useful to advise her to prepare for leaving by making sure she has some or all of the following ready to hand: birth certificates; benefit books; savings books; driving licence; jewellery; photos.

- If the woman leaves, *never* agree to contact the woman on the man's behalf. This lets him know you know where she is, and could lead to a breach of confidence.

- If you are approached by the man, don't be fooled by a pleasant manner or appearance. Most women who do leave are more at risk of rape or murder after they have left the abusive relationship.

- *Never* give the man the address or phone number of where she is staying.

- Be careful where you meet the woman. Always be conscious that the abusive man may be watching you.

CHAPTER 5

The outreach worker's survival guide

'Therefore since we are surrounded by such a great cloud of witnesses, let us throw off everything that hinders and the sin that so easily entangles, and let us run with perseverance the race marked out for us. Let us fix our eyes on Jesus, the author and perfecter of our faith, who for the joy set before him, endured the cross, scorning its shame, and sat down at the right hand of the throne of God. Consider him who endured such opposition from sinful men, so that you will not grow weary and lose heart.'

(Hebrews 12:1–3)

In this chapter we will give you some hints and guidelines as to how you can deal with some of the problems which you may encounter as you reach out to people who work in the sex industry. First, we will look at ways for you to stick together as a team and then we will look at avoiding burnout, which is very common in all kinds of mission work. Then, we will consider two common hazards for those working with people – emotional dependency and manipulation.

5.1   Sticking together

One of Satan's main ploys in destroying any kind of effective mission is to drive a wedge between those who are doing the work. It is essential that you work hard for unity within your team. Here are some guidelines.

- Set up continuing training for the team to cover the areas which are important for its work. Build up a library of useful books and resources, eg on evangelism, health issues, spirituality and so on. This is a good time to link up with other teams – you could have training days together. Don't work in isolation and don't try to reinvent the wheel when someone else is already doing the work! Theological colleges and established mission agencies will provide classes and good material.

- We suggest that you try to go on a team retreat regularly, say three times a year. At these meetings, aim for honesty and integrity. Discuss team aims and values, as well as having fun and relaxing.

- Make a commitment to resolve team conflict as and when it happens.

- Review what you are doing. Ask yourselves what you are doing well. What are your strengths and weaknesses? What could you do better? Are you still holding to your vision?

- Make sure you continue to pray as a team, asking God for grace, wisdom, discernment, faith and understanding in your work, as well as openings to be able to meet and talk to the girls.

5.2   Avoiding burnout

In the last chapter we emphasised that perseverance is required. We stressed that relationships take a long time to build up and that you may not always see the fruits of your labours. We also stressed that continuity and consistency are very important. In other words, in order to build up relationships with the women, you have to go out regularly, even when you don't feel like it. They need to know that you are reliable, because very little else in their lives will be.

With this in mind, many people start out in Christian service with great intentions. They feel called by God, and rightly think that if God wants them to do something He will give them the strength to do it. However, many people do not persevere, and there is a high drop-out rate among full-time workers and volunteers in Christian mission. Why is this? It could be that some simply lose interest. It could be that some can't be bothered any more. Others find that family or work commitments mean that they are unable to devote the time to the work which they would like. However, the majority of people drop out because they find it difficult to cope with the extra stresses this work has brought into their lives. They find that they are unable to carry on with the work that God has called them to do and in the end they feel worthless and as if they are a failure. And often the reason for this is that they have taken on too much and become completely exhausted and unable to function. They have allowed 'busyness' to be more important than obedience, and have suffered from burnout. In other words, they simply have been unable to achieve a balance in which they remain spiritually, emotionally and physically healthy, and they have felt the need to withdraw from their work, feeling unable to cope with all that they feel they should be doing. How can this be avoided?

Spiritual health

The key here is intimacy with the Father. Make use of the prayer support we have suggested in Chapter 3. Also make sure your own relationship with Jesus is kept fresh by reading your Bible prayerfully and talking regularly to Him. Of course, there are lots of Christian books that can help you with this.

It is also important that you stay in regular fellowship with other believers, and are involved in your own church. Many of you may have full-time jobs, or have families to care for, as well as your commitment to outreach. Others will be in full-time outreach work. Whatever category you are in, as the ministry grows, you may begin to wonder how you can possibly find time to pray and do all that you have to do. Very often the busier you are, the less time you may allocate for prayer – it becomes low on your list of priorities. We have found that if you begin your day with prayer, you will get through much more than you thought you would. Your work will become much more effective if you spend time in private prayer every day, not just regarding your own concerns, but interceding for other people.

Physical health

Besides the usual important things such as balanced diet and taking exercise, perhaps the most important piece of advice we can give is to make sure you get adequate rest. In Christian work there is a tendency to take on too much, believing that it is the Lord's will that you take on everything you are asked to do. There is a well-recognised tendency among Christians to be unable to know their own limitations, to take on too much, or simply to refuse to rest. Many Christians find it very difficult to say no when they are asked to do things. It is crucial, however, that you take seriously the biblical principle of doing no work on one day of the week. Jesus Himself knew the importance of rest, and made sure that He had times alone with God.

Emotional health

The principle of rest also applies to maintaining your emotional health. If you take adequate rest and don't clog up your life with constant activity, you will find that you are better able to cope with the stress of outreach. If you know your limitations, and are able to say 'no' to requests to take on more commitments, you will find your stress levels remain healthy. Knowing your limitations does not mean that you are no longer relying on God's strength, it is merely learning at what point you should withdraw. In this way you will be far more effective than if you take on too much and become bad-tempered, complaining and bitter, have sudden explosive outbursts of temper, or feel unable to make decisions – all of which are signs of burnout. A key warning sign that the risk of burnout is increasing is if you start thinking that you are the only one who can do this job, that the project will collapse without you, and that you are the only one who does things properly. We're not yet in the age to come, so perfectionism should not be a part of your view of yourself.

5.3　Dealing with manipulation

One of the biggest hazards of working with any group of people is the risk of being manipulated. This means that the person you are caring for is controlling you, manipulating how you deal with her, and making sure that she gets what she wants out of the relationship.

In many walks of life you may be aware of being manipulated by another person. More often, however, you will not be aware of the fact that you are being manipulated – precisely because you are being manipulated! Some people do this quite openly, by threatening and bullying. However, real manipulation is when someone attempts to control in a much more subtle way. The manipulative person will try to get you to do what he or she wants. But you are there to do what God wants.

Here are some good examples of behaviour which may be described as manipulative:

- Giving gifts for no good reason

- Eye contact – meaningful looks, refusing to look at another when displeased, flattery, eg 'I don't know what I'd do without you'; 'You are the best outreach worker on the team,' and so on (Proverbs 29:5)

- Private jokes – exclusive talk

- Exaggerating needs in order to gain sympathy

- Making the other person feel guilty – 'You wouldn't do that if you really cared for me.'

- Cold silences

- Playing one member of the team against another [1]

These are some of the things to watch out for as you build up relationships with the women. Recognising manipulation is a matter of experience, often painful. Some people have an instinct which tells them when they are being manipulated, others are less able to spot the signs. Do take the advice of others, and make your relationships with the women a matter of prayer. If you find yourself responding to a request by saying, 'It goes against my better judgment, but...', stop and think who is in control of the situation and whether it is in fact a good idea to say 'yes' to a particular request, or respond to the kind of behaviour outlined above, in the way that the woman intends.

5.4 Guarding against co-dependency

Part of your work is to build up relationships with the women you meet. This is a risky business – you are opening up yourself to be hurt. The following is provided to help you to see some warning signs of when a relationship is becoming unhealthy. It is possible for one or the other, or even both parties, to become too emotionally dependent on that relationship. Don't be misled, the guidelines are not simply for you to watch out for certain behaviours in the woman, but to watch out for in yourself. This again is where you should be honest with the other team members and your support group, and allow them to help you through difficulties. Others can often see problems arising where you can't. It is characteristic of many Christian workers that they become blinkered in what they do, and are unable to listen and accept criticism from one another. Remember, all criticism can be used for good: you can learn from it. And just because you are criticised does not mean that the person criticising you no longer holds you in high regard. Learn to listen

---

[1] Most of this list is adapted from the section on manipulation in Lori Thorkelson's book *Counselling the Homosexual* which is listed in the Suggestions for Further Reading section.

to others and don't camouflage your own fears and anxieties, stubbornness or self-will, and don't attempt to manipulate by insisting that the Lord has told you to do something. Scripture says that the spirits must be tested, and that all ministry and service is a matter of mutual support.

This brings us on to the need to set boundaries in all that you do. Learning to know your limitations is one way to set boundaries, so that your life is not completely taken over by the work and the needs of the women. It is useful to learn that saying 'no' does not necessarily mean a lack of love on your part. Keeping your own privacy is as important as getting adequate time off.

Learning the importance of setting boundaries and recognising the signs of manipulation are important ways of helping to guard against co-dependency. This happens when your motivation for becoming involved in people's lives becomes distorted, and your relationship with a woman becomes important for your well-being.

Melody Beattie [2] defines a co-dependent person as follows:

'A person who has let someone else's behaviour affect him or her and is obsessed with controlling other people's behaviour.'

Co-dependency is a common reaction in people who live or work with alcoholics or drug addicts. They become completely taken up with trying to stop the addict behaving in certain destructive ways. In other words, they try to take on responsibility for the person. This is clearly against biblical teaching, in which it is made clear that everyone is responsible for his or her own actions.

Part and parcel of this wrong way of thinking (ie that you are responsible for the other person's behaviour) is the danger of becoming emotionally dependent on the person for whom you are caring. That is to say, the relationship, and your helping role in it, becomes an important part of your life on which you become dependent. This tends to happen to people who have a need to be needed. Such people need to have someone to help, and often the relationship becomes more important for the helper's well-being than it is for the person who is being helped. In these cases, when the relationship ends, it is often far more upsetting for the helper than the client. This is a dangerous situation to be in, and is a prime cause of the burnout we were talking about earlier. Once again we would urge that you talk about your work with other members of the team, be open to positive criticism, and take the advice of others.

Here are some further warning signs of possible co-dependency:

■ being unable to see the other's faults realistically;

■ becoming defensive about the relationship;

---

[2] Melody Beattie's important book on co-dependency, *Co-Dependent No More*, on which we have drawn heavily here, is highly recommended for further reading.

- not wanting to share ministry in the relationship with anyone else;

- becoming preoccupied with the person;

- other relationships suffer;

- speaking for the other person without consulting them;

- making decisions for them;

- wanting to be liked;

- too upset when there is a cooling off.

As we said at the beginning of this chapter, dealing with people is a risky business. You may well be hurt. However, we have a friend who is never unreliable, who never lets us down or hurts us in any way. He never changes, and His love for us is beyond our comprehension. He is the one on whom we should be dependent – no human being can take the strain! Hallelujah!

> 'The LORD is my strength and my song;
>   he has become my salvation.
> He is my God, and I will praise him,
>   my father's God, and I will exalt him.'
>
> (Exodus 15:2)

Case study

A right dependency

When she was 16, Gina left home to escape her father who had sexually abused her for many years. Sometimes she slept rough, sometimes she lived in hostels. One day a friend in the hostel suggested that she could make some money by working the streets. Gina became addicted to alcohol and pills which she took in order to dull the pain of working. She took a massive overdose and nearly died. After that she became severely depressed, was sectioned and kept in hospital for many months. During her time in hospital she began to pray and ask God for help. Six years later, Gina is still following Jesus. She still has flashbacks and nightmares because of the abuse, but is finding that counselling helps her not to find help from drugs or alcohol but to persevere in her walk with God.

PART 2

CHAPTER 6

Health issues

'Surely he took up our infirmities
    and carried our sorrows,
yet we considered him stricken by God,
    smitten by him and afflicted.
But he was pierced for our transgressions,
    he was crushed for our iniquities;
the punishment that brought us peace was upon him,
    and by his wounds we are healed.'

(Isaiah 53:4–5)

6.1 Prostitution and health

Sex workers are very prone to ill health

This is primarily because of the unhealthy nature of their work – the more clients they have, the more likely they are to become infected with everything from the common cold to the AIDS virus. The risk of serious illness is greatly increased if prostitution is combined with drug or alcohol abuse.[1] The chaotic lifestyle which tends to accompany prostitution, plus the distorted self-image which results from selling sex, tends also to result in high instances of mental illness among prostitutes. This could be anything from mild anxiety, through depression, to a full-blown psychosis in which the worker loses all sense of reality.

The aim here is to provide you with general information about the major health problems associated with prostitution, and to enable you to help the women with whom you work to minimise the risk of serious illness. Some sex workers can be reluctant to go to the doctor, perhaps out of fear of what might be discovered, or perhaps because they see the doctor as an unwelcome authority figure who may try to disrupt their lives. In inner-city areas, clinics and drop-in centres are set up specifically for sex workers. If there is one in your area get to know the staff and encourage the women to make use of this service, which is designed to cater for their needs. An alternative to the general practitioner (GP) is well-woman clinics.

Sometimes, you may find that you are faced with an emergency, such as a drug overdose or serious wounding. We have included some guidelines for action in certain situations, but there is no doubt that it is invaluable for you to become a qualified first-aider. Training for this is available from organisations such as the Red Cross and St John's Ambulance.

> *'Yet the news about him spread all the more, so that crowds of people came to hear him and be healed of their sicknesses.'*
>
> (Luke 5:15)

6.2 God's plan

Physical and mental illness are part of our fallen world. The Gospels record that Jesus healed the sick, and that He told the disciples that they too would heal and perform miracles. There is no doubt that Jesus still heals miraculously today. We have experience of God doing marvellous healings among

---

[1] Further information on the health risks associated with drug abuse is given in the sections on 'Hepatitis B, C and D' (page 71) and 'Protection for outreach workers' (page 71), and in Chapter 8: 'Addiction' (page 85).

the women. For example, we know of some who have been miraculously freed from drug addiction, with no need for detox or rehabilitation.

However, a word of warning is necessary concerning your attitude towards signs and wonders. In obedience to Christ, it should be part of your ministry to bring the women's health problems (and those of their families and friends) before the Lord. Undoubtedly, you will see wonderful things happen; but the answers to your prayers may not necessarily be 'miraculous', and some people may not be healed.

Remember that although Jesus healed many, there were far more whom He did not heal. God works in many different ways. Often, watching someone change slowly through the gracious working of the Holy Spirit is just as amazing and wonderful as any sign or wonder would be. In other words, don't expect God to work in any particular way – His methods belong to Him, and Him alone. If you experience signs and wonders – praise God, but try to avoid focusing on these 'results' rather than on Him. Keep your eyes on Jesus, and remember His frequent instructions to those He healed not to publicise what had happened to them. He did not want to be thought of merely as a wonder worker, and He did not want the healing to be glorified rather than God Himself. If you don't see any miracles, and you find that this troubles you, you may well be missing all the other marvellous things which God is doing in your lives and those of the women with whom you are working!

6.3 Physical health problems associated with prostitution

Increased risk of infection

Drug-users are very prone to infection generally. Infections should not be ignored, because the women's general immunity and ability to fight off infection tends to be lessened. In particular, it is common for injection sites to become infected, and abscesses may form. This could lead to gangrene and the danger of losing the affected limb. Another risk is septicaemia (blood poisoning) which, in turn could damage the valves of the heart. The risk of infection is greatly reduced if clean needles are always used for each individual dose. Find out where clean needles are avaiable in your area; make sure the women know about this service, and encourage them to use it.

Sex workers are also more likely to become infected with sexually transmitted diseases (STDs) such as genital warts or herpes, and gonorrhoea. Symptoms of STDs include blisters, warts, ulcers in the genital area, lower abdominal pain, and vaginal discharge. The most common infection is chlamydia, which can lead to pelvic inflammatory disease, fertility problems and an increased risk of ectopic pregnancy (in which the fertilised egg implants itself in the fallopian tube, rather than in the wall of the uterus). The most feared infection, however, is AIDS, which will be considered in greater depth below. Confidential treatment is available at the genito-urinary departments of general hospitals and specialised clinics. It is useful to find out where these are, know their addresses and telephone numbers and what the referral procedure is.

Increased risk of cervical cancer

The predisposing factors for cervical cancer are:

- multiple sexual partners;

- early experience of sexual intercourse;

- smoking;

- low socio-economic class;

- human papilloma (a subtype of which causes genital warts).

It will be clear from this that prostitutes run a very high risk of cervical cancer. As you build up a relationship with the women, try to encourage them to attend regularly for cervical smear tests.

HIV

HIV (human immunodeficiency virus) is the virus responsible for AIDS (acquired immune deficiency syndrome). HIV attacks a particular type of cell in the blood stream known as a lymphocyte, which is responsible for the body's immune system.

The virus is spread by intimate contact of bodily fluids (blood, saliva and semen). It can be transmitted sexually, and by contact with blood or blood products (eg in the use of contaminated needles used intravenously or through transfusions). It may also be passed from mother to child within the womb. In the UK, the main sources of infection are the sharing of needles among drug-users and unprotected sex, whether heterosexual or homo-sexual.

Most people who test positive for HIV go on to develop full-blown AIDS. When this develops, the body becomes less able to fight infection. Common symptoms of AIDS include:

- cough, which may be due to chest infection or pneumonia;

- general malaise, weakness and fever symptoms;

- pruritus (itching), perhaps due to dry skin or scabies;

- diarrhoea;

◼ anorexia (loss of appetite) and vomiting, perhaps due to malignancy or candida infection.

The progress of the AIDS virus is variable and therefore unpredictable. Sometimes the symptoms outlined above can show up very quickly, but for some, manifestations of illness may not appear until some time after detection of the virus. However, after the symptoms of AIDS appear, the average survival time is reckoned to be 18–30 months. As the disease develops, many different problems can appear, such as infections, malignancies and neurological disease and muscle wasting. The person will require skilled nursing care and sensitive medical treatment as the illness progresses.

Despite much research, there is still no cure for AIDS, although medication can help to control symptoms and improve the patient's quality of life. At present, the main weapons in tackling this disease (which has reached epidemic proportions in Africa and Asia) are prevention and control through health education.

It is estimated that most female sex workers who contract HIV have a five-year lifespan. In particular, intravenous drug-users' general health and immunity tend to be low. Treatment may be made more difficult because of the poor condition of the drug user's veins. If a woman you are working with seems ill, and unable to shake off infections, don't be afraid to mention HIV testing – she will probably have thought of this herself and be relieved to have the issue brought into the open. If possible, make sure that she is accompanied to hospitals and clinics. This will help offset the rejection which she may experience from other people.

If a woman asks for advice as to whether or not she should be tested for HIV, find out why she is considering it. If she has valid reasons for wanting to be tested, and you feel that she could cope with hearing a bad result, then encourage her to have a test. However, if she is merely responding to peer group or professional pressure (for example, from social workers or nurses), seems generally well, and you feel she could not cope with a positive diagnosis, then we suggest you advise her not to take the test. We have seen women who get a bad result become extremely depressed and even suicidal. We have also seen women who have become so angry about their diagnosis that they adopt an even more promiscuous lifestyle. So, if the woman seems healthy, and has no good reason to have a test, we recommend that she does not have one. Do, however, take advice from your team and support group.

It is also worth noting that negative results from an HIV test can be unreliable, because it can take up to three months for the virus to become detectable in the blood stream. On the other hand, positive tests are very reliable.

Working with someone who has HIV can be very difficult and stressful. The person needs to learn to grieve, to accept the situation and not to deny it. There is a need to set priorities in life, and to make the most of the help which is available. Besides the medical problems outlined above, AIDS sufferers also need committed emotional and spiritual support from the time of diagnosis through to death. Usually, in terminal care, the role of the carer is to support the family as they care for their relative. The very nature of AIDS, however, makes care much more complex. In the first place, the woman may not have any support networks on which to rely, perhaps because of her chaotic lifestyle or because of illness or addiction in the family. It is also possible for other members of the family to be infected with the disease and, consequently, for any support network which does exist to be severely overloaded. Another complicating factor in the care of AIDS sufferers is the infectious nature of the disease, which induces fear on the part of possible carers and can result in the person being socially isolated. This may be compounded by stigma and fear surrounding STDs or drug involvement, which can lead to the woman being shunned by her family.

If you find that you are supporting a woman with HIV/AIDS, make sure you have your own support networks firmly in place. This will help you to keep spiritually and emotionally afloat. Try to learn as much as you can about how to care for someone with HIV/AIDS and do not work in isolation. Organisations such as ACET[2] can support the carer as well as the sufferer, and you should make use of their expertise. In this book we cannot give a complete guide to the care of AIDS sufferers, but we can give some guidelines for ministry.

- A particular problem may be apathy. The woman may think there is no point in changing her lifestyle when she is going to die anyway. For example, if she is a drug-user, it may seem easier for her to stay in her own environment where she feels accepted and safe, than to go to a rehabilitation centre, be challenged to change, and learn new life skills. However, it is important to deal with the underlying drug problem or emotional pain of working before dealing with the impact of the virus in her life. Only then is the woman able to see the situation in proper perspective and to face up to the question of her own mortality. She cannot do this if she is running away from reality in any way. In the early stages of the illness, it is far more important for her to learn to deal with her own grief and hopes for the future than to deal with society's inability to accept the 'abnormal'. Explain that a chaotic lifestyle will exacerbate the virus.

- Try to work through family problems with her. Try to help her re-establish contact with her family if this has been lost, and if the rebuilding of relationships will be beneficial to her.

- Help her to see things positively. Has she any ambitions she would like to achieve, eg taking an art course? Her quality of life will be much better if she sees what she can do, rather than what she can't do, with her life.

---

[2] ACET (AIDS Care Education & Training), PO Box 3693, London, SW15 2BS. E-mail: acet@acetuk.org Website: www.acetuk.org

- Encourage her to become involved in organisations and specialist care for those who are HIV-positive. Encourage her to attend specialised clinics.

- Be sensitive to confidentiality. Discuss with the woman whom she wants to be informed of her illness, and respect her wishes.

- Be with her. Remember the words of Christ: *'I was sick and you looked after me'* (Matthew 25:36). Give concentrated support when she is first diagnosed and then back down slightly, in order to prevent an over-dependent relationship forming.

- Pray with her. Discuss the illness with her as well as the possibility of death. Try to help her not to react to the pain of the illness, and all that it entails, with bitterness, rebellion or unforgiveness, because these will only make her pain greater. Help her to learn to love – perfect love casts out all fear. Above all, keep assuring her of Christ's love for her, and pray that she will see that love through you and other believers.

Hepatitis B, C and D

The hepatitis viruses cause severe infection of the liver. Like AIDS, these are blood-borne infections, and can be spread through unprotected sex or the sharing of needles. They carry a high risk of resulting in severe liver disease such as cirrhosis or cancer. Although not everyone who is infected goes on to contract liver disease, they may be carriers (ie people who have the virus but who do not show symptoms of the disease) and so might still infect others. This group of diseases constitutes as great a risk to the general population as the HIV virus.

The first symptoms of hepatitis are fever, tiredness, nausea, loss of appetite and general weakness. There may also be diarrhoea and vomiting. However, the main symptom of hepatitis is jaundice (a yellow tinge in the skin and in the whites of the eyes), which may (but not always) appear one to two weeks after these symptoms have stopped and the person is feeling better. A three-dose vaccination course can protect your team against hepatitis B and it is essential that you are familiar with, and carry out, the preventative measures given here (see *Protection for outreach workers* below). At present no vaccine has been developed for hepatitis C and D.

6.4   Protection for outreach workers

It is essential that your team members protect themselves against both HIV and the hepatitis virus. Here are some basic precautions which should be taken to protect staff from hepatitis and HIV:

- ▓ Cover all cuts, however minor, with a waterproof plaster.

- ▓ Wear disposable gloves when there is a chance of coming into contact with body fluids.

- ▓ Use disposable towels to clear up spillages of body fluids, together with household bleach if necessary.

- ▓ Ensure that clothes and bedlinen which are stained with blood, semen, vomit, and so on, are washed immediately, using the washing machine's hot cycle.

- ▓ If there is a major spillage of blood, burn the contaminated clothing, if possible. Alternatively, place the clothes in two polythene bags labelled 'CONTAMINATED CLOTHING' and arrange for disposal by your local council. Always avoid touching the clothes with your bare hands.

- ▓ Good hygiene and vaccinations will ensure that all staff are properly protected against the small, but significant, risk of infection.

- ▓ It is recommended that all members of the outreach team are vaccinated against hepatitis B. The vaccination can be done by your GP.

- ▓ If any member of your team receives a needlestick injury from a used syringe needle, and has not been vaccinated against hepatitis B, he or she should seek medical help immediately.

6.5   Related issues

Children and HIV

Babies who have the HIV virus have had their destiny decided before they can make any choices about their lives. The bondage of a previous generation has been passed on to them and they are already slaves to the illness. This should spur us on to minister to those adults who are most at risk and bring the hurts to the Great Healer. In this way they may be dealt with before a lifestyle affects the innocent next generation.

The issue of whether or not testing for the virus is an appropriate course is very different when children are involved. If the mother develops symptoms it is essential that the child be tested immediately. If a woman has a child who contracts the disease, she often feels an overwhelming sense of failure as a parent. If this crisis develops, the best way a team can help is once again simply by being there, helping with practical things such as taking the child to the clinic, and providing a listening ear.

Not all children of HIV-positive parents contract the virus. Equally, the virus can take some years to surface in a child; there may be a negative test at two years old, and a positive one at, say, four years old.

When a mother is unable to face reality for fear of pain, she needs to be challenged with the fact that this is selfish as far as her children are concerned. She needs to be able to plan for her children's future, to see that the failure is not in being ill but in denying her HIV status and neglecting her children. Denial and guilt cause stress which merely exacerbates the illness.

Condoms and contraception

Most sex workers contract HIV through intravenous drug use and not through sex. Sex workers mostly practise 'safe sex' by using condoms. They are perhaps most at risk of contracting the virus in prison where there is often a shortage of syringes. Always advise women to use condoms and to have a supply with them as they work. Some may be allergic to condoms, and experience soreness in the vagina; anti-allergenic condoms are available at clinics. As we have already said, your team will have to work out whether or not it is right to distribute condoms to the women. Certainly, you should know where the women can obtain condoms and encourage them to use this service. Be aware, however, that while the women themselves may want to use condoms, some of their clients may not, and may pay extra for unprotected sex.

Using condoms helps guard against other STDs and hepatitis B, and it reduces the risk of pregnancy. It is advisable, however, for sex workers to use other forms of contraception too. If there is any fear of pregnancy, for example, if a condom bursts or has not been used, it may be possible (if this option is morally acceptable to the woman) to get the emergency contraceptive pill from a GP or family planning clinic. This is usually a series of tablets which should be started within 72 hours of intercourse.

Abortion

Most prostitutes have had at least one abortion. The use of contraceptives is so much a part of their working lives that they do not tend to use them in their private relationships. Many will have had their first pregnancy aborted because they were under age. Other pregnancies may have been terminated because the woman was afraid of being declared an unfit mother by the authorities and having the child taken away from her. Women perceive this as rejection, and the fear of this can be so great that the women would rather decide the fate of their own children than have someone else decide for them.

Following an abortion, the woman may feel hopeless. She may see herself as powerless to break the vicious circle she has got into. This may be made worse if she has come from a dysfunctional background in which she has had a bad relationship with her own mother. This means that she will not have the resources to understand what true mothering is about. She has no-one to turn to for advice.

The view taken here is that abortion is a sin – against the will of God. It is important that we be seen to hate the sin, but love the sinner. If a woman who is pregnant comes to you for help, don't give advice in a way that will put pressure on her. Listen to her, believe in her, and show that you care for her. If you pressurise her to keep the baby she will probably rebel. Pray with her and ask the Holy Spirit to bring truth into the situation. Remember that the choice is hers – don't tell her what to do. Discuss the situation and the options with her. Try to seek a solution to the practical problems in a way that will encourage her to continue with the pregnancy. However, if she chooses to have an abortion, stand committed to her while she goes through with it. It is probably better not to go to the hospital with her when she has her termination, but give her lots of support afterwards.

6.6 Mental health (and ill health)

The human mind is not able to cope with the abuse of the body which working as a prostitute entails. Our bodies are made in the image of God and are meant to be temples of the Holy Spirit. So, when sex workers are continually subjected to invasion and abuse, they are bound to become psychologically wounded. They become alienated from God and from that which He intended them to be. In this situation the mind cries out to be understood and to be quiet and still. However, as long as the vicious cycle of working continues, constant activity drowns out these cries of pain and the wounds become deeper and deeper. A combination of past experience (prior to working) and the effects of working itself can cause mental confusion and the need for psychiatric help.

Many sex workers do become depressed as a result of their lifestyle. Most, however, will manage to disguise this, hiding it from themselves and others by filling their lives with endless activity, most of which will simply add further problems to those they have already. Most women will tell you that they do not want to be doing the work that they do, and very few will have any self-esteem at all. Many will speak of suicide, feeling a sense of hopelessness. They know that they would feel better about themselves if they changed their lifestyles but do not know how to do this. They need the renewed hope that only Jesus can bring.

Sometimes a woman may have had a history of mental illness before she started her career in prostitution. For example, she may suffer from anorexia nervosa (in which she diets to lose weight to such an extent that she may put her life in danger) or bulimia (in which she has episodes of bingeing on food which she then gets rid of by vomiting). Or she may suffer from uncontrolled mood swings (eg as in manic depression). During a period of elation she may become sexually disinhibited, her sexuality going out of control. Unrestrained, violent outbursts may make her even more socially isolated. The excessive sexual activity of this period may leave her with profound feelings of guilt as she enters a more depressed phase.

The lives of sex workers can be so complex and chaotic that sometimes it can be difficult to establish what is reality and what is not. For example, drug-users and alcoholics can become anxious and paranoid, and believe that people are out to get them, when this is not the case. On the other hand the women tend to lead such chaotic lives and have less-than-stable, if not dangerous, relationships with pimps and clients, that what may sound unusual and even unbelievable to us is in fact the reality of their lives. Women may be in genuine fear of people who have a grudge against them.

Usually, those who suffer from mental illness are well known to the psychiatric services. It is essential that this contact and the treatment prescribed by the consultant psychiatrist be adhered to. Mental illness may make the woman very much more vulnerable to assault and abuse from both clients and pimps, as their judgment of danger and risk may be impaired. Someone who is mentally ill may have no perception of how physically ill she may be, or have little insight into abnormal or bizarre behaviour which draws attention to her vulnerability. Where possible, and with the permission of the woman, liaise with psychiatric workers involved in the case. This will help ensure that there is continuity of care.

Do try to learn about mental illness, its symptoms and its causes. If you think it is appropriate, do pray with the woman, but be wary of anyone who wants to try to 'cast out the demon of mental illness'. Untold damage has been done by those who have taken this line and have completely misunderstood the nature of psychiatric problems. Not only will you lose the respect of secular agencies, you may well do much damage in the process.

Case study

Spiral downhill

Madeleine is 26 years old and uses heroin. She has worked the streets for a number of years in order to support her drug habit. Now, however, she has had to stop working because of ill health. Madeleine had been injecting her drugs into her stomach because the veins in her arms and legs had collapsed. She developed an abscess which had to be lanced by the doctor, but septicaemia set in.

Madeleine's family circumstances mean that she cannot rely on close relatives for support. Her mother and brother both died through drug abuse. She lives with her elder sister who works the streets, is on drugs, and has developed AIDS.

CHAPTER 7

Sexuality

'Do not judge, or you too will be judged.'
(Matthew 7:1)

7.1   The biblical attitude to sex

Throughout Christian history believers have stressed the need for sexual purity, and have focused on what we should not do as far as sexual activity is concerned. They have tended to give rules about sexual behaviour which are certainly biblical, but they have not thought about why these rules are there in the first place. As we shall see below, the instructions and commandments are given for our good, and for our freedom, not simply because of some abstract morality principle, or merely for the sake of limiting our behaviour.

One result of this prohibitive way of thinking has been to increase a judgmental tendency, against which Jesus explicitly speaks. For example, it has contributed to an attitude in which those who find it easy to live a sexually pure life look down on those who find it more difficult. But more than this, it has led to an unhealthy emphasis on sexual sin, and to viewing sexual behaviour as the primary gauge of a person's spiritual health.

This emphasis, however, is far from biblical. Sexual sin is only one sin among many others. When, after the Fall, men and women became rebellious, God gave us up to all sorts of sin, allowing us to do what we wanted, giving us over to a 'depraved mind' (Romans 1:28). It is true that such sin includes sexual sin, but Paul makes it clear that sexual sin is only one part of that depravity: deceit, fraud, gossip and arrogance are deemed to be just as bad (Romans 1:29ff). In Galatians, too, sexual sin is only one sin among many:

> 'The acts of the sinful nature are obvious: sexual immorality, impurity and debauchery; idolatry and witchcraft; hatred, discord, jealousy, fits of rage, selfish ambition, dissensions, factions and envy; drunkenness, orgies, and the like. I warn you, as I did before, that those who live like this will not inherit the kingdom of God.'
> (Galatians 5:19–21)

Which of us is able to say that we are not guilty of selfish ambition or envy? It is precisely because we all have the tendency to sin, and because we all do sin, that Jesus says that none of us has the right to condemn another. As He says to those about to punish the woman taken in adultery,

> 'If any one of you is without sin, let him be the first to throw a stone at her.'
> (John 8:7)

He commands a compassionate approach which lifts people out of their sin rather than a condemning one which very often serves to drive them further away from the Church and from God.

The apostle Paul speaks straightforwardly about sex. Quite simply, anything outside monogamous marriage is seen as wrong. Today, many readers of the Bible see the prescriptions against all kinds of promiscuity as restricting people's freedom. Much of the 20th-century sexual revolution has been a revolt against this perceived curtailing of our liberty. In fact, however,

God has given these commandments for our freedom, for our well-being. Our loving heavenly Father knows that disobedience actually opens up the way for Satan to destroy our lives. We only have to look at the immense damage done to children of families torn apart by adultery, for example. Similarly, unwanted pregnancies, broken relationships and much disease would be avoided if we obeyed our Father's will on this matter. His intention is not to deny us pleasure, but to ensure that sex is enjoyed in the safety of an intimate relationship. But why should promiscuity cause such damage in the first place?

In the Bible, the human body is not just a physical entity. It houses the human spirit and, for the believer, it also houses the Holy Spirit (1 Corinthians 6:9). The body contains the heart (the seat of all emotions) and the mind, which includes the will. As far as believers are concerned, our bodies are also part of the Body of Christ, functioning as His representatives on earth as well as being closely and intimately linked with each other. What we do affects not only ourselves but others in the Church. But this does not answer the question as to why our sexual behaviour should be curtailed, especially since sexuality is a good gift from God. The fact is that what we do with our bodies directly affects our personal well-being. The apostle Paul tells us,

'All other sins a man commits are outside his body, but he who sins sexually sins against his own body.'   (1 Corinthians 6:18)

This verse tells us that there is a close link between our actions and our personal identity.

The Bible does not teach a dualistic view of the body. In other words, it does not teach that there is a gulf between our physical bodies and our mental or emotional capacities. On the contrary, the two are inseparable and intertwined. This means that whatever we do with our bodies affects our emotions, our minds and our whole selves, our spirits. Consequently, sex cannot be seen as a purely physical thing – sexual activity cannot be divorced from all other kinds of activity, and it affects every other aspect of our lives and well-being.

Sex is not only a physical and emotional matter, it is also spiritual. Genesis 2:24 tells us that when two people have a sexual relationship they become 'one flesh'. Each time sexual intercourse takes place, two bodies are literally united and can be said to be one flesh. However, because flesh and spirit cannot be separated, something happens between the two people which binds them to each other and means that each one has somehow been affected by the encounter. They do not merely give each other their bodies, they also somehow (mysteriously) give something of their own inner being, their own spirit.

Once this mystery is acknowledged, we can see why God has prescribed monogamy as the best way for human sexuality to be expressed. For, if people are promiscuous, and having sexual relations with many people, they are effectively giving away part of themselves and receiving parts of others. If this happens too often, they are effectively doing violence to their inner being or soul, and the personality becomes fragmented. This is indeed what we see in many prostitutes. They no longer know who they are, have little or no self-esteem, and have no sense of their value as an individual. In a word, they have no sense of self.

We can see now why the Bible is against prostitution, and indeed any form of promiscuity. It involves the wrong and careless use of the body which God has created, and therefore harms the individuals concerned. It brings about physical, spiritual and emotional disease. It has a violent effect on the created spirit of humanity which is housed within a physical body, and if the person concerned is a believer, it has an effect on the entire Body of Christ.

For sex workers who continue in their promiscuous lifestyle, there can be no way in which the simple and straightforward way of life advocated by the Bible can be realised. On the contrary, life becomes increasingly complicated, confused and painful. You will find that some women have become confused about their sexuality because of their activity as prostitutes. For example, some women who have worked for many years have come to despise and distrust men, and turn to other women to have their sexual and emotional needs met. Others will have adopted a bi-sexual lifestyle. Still others will have had some kind of sexual confusion in their lives even before they started work as prostitutes, the heartache and loneliness simply being compounded and made worse by the work they do.

7.2   Sexual confusion

Within sex workers' culture there may be a high degree of lesbian promiscuity. The women are always searching for love. Loneliness in prison, bad experiences with men, and a strong loyalty among the women can all contribute to a lesbian lifestyle. There can also be a good deal of violence within such relationships as jealousies and quarrels develop.

The longer a woman is involved in working the more likely she is to adopt lesbian behaviour patterns as she seeks love and gentleness in her life. For some, sexual behaviour is determined by circumstances. For example, a woman may be lesbian while in prison, but may stop this when she is released. A 'triangular' relationship between a woman, her lesbian lover and her pimp is not uncommon, and may serve to fulfil some of her needs for close relationships. In some cases, the woman works to provide drugs for the more dominant 'male' lesbian partner. In situations like this, the partner could almost be seen as a pimp. The woman may feel that she is being a homemaker, looking after her partner. By the same token, the 'male' partner may perceive herself as looking after her woman. However, those involved in lesbian relationships may well feel a sense of frustration. They have a natural desire to be protected and provided for by a man. Ultimately, sex cannot silence the cry for a true identity.

Bisexuality is common among sex workers. It is part and parcel of the confusion and slackening of boundaries which characterise the chaotic lifestyle. As dissatisfaction with their own sexuality grows, and as their emotional hurts increase, they may seek love from both men and women. However, they will most probably find that this does not satisfy completely. It is very unusual to meet a prostitute who is either purely heterosexual or exclusively lesbian.

Rent boys' private lives are often promiscuous as they try to fulfil their love needs. Like many other men they dream of meeting someone they can care for and provide for, and to give them a life of tranquillity. This may be worked out in a distorted way in their relationships with clients, other rent boys, and their pimps. Equally, however, it is not uncommon for rent boys to have heterosexual relationships outside their working lives, and to see their sexual activities at work as purely functional with no emotional aspect whatsoever.

Pointers for ministry

It is important to have both men and women on a team which is to deal with matters of sexual confusion. It is very healing for a homosexual or lesbian to be ministered to by a heterosexual. Often, they have a deep longing for an in-depth platonic relationship with someone of their own sex. However, women ministering to homosexual men should be self-aware. It is common for women to feel safe when working with homosexual men, and to hug or kiss them in ways which would be inappropriate with heterosexual men. This affirms the dysfunction rather than challenging it, and may even be indicative of a woman's need to feel safe within a male relationship rather than anything else. In supervision and in prayer, self-examination and challenging of motives is essential when ministering to the sexually hurt.

For those women who make a decision to follow Jesus, and who have become involved in homosexual relationships as part of their promiscuous lifestyles, good discipleship is an essential part of healing. Believers can show the love of Jesus and bring truth and light into the person's pain and darkness. They can demonstrate that it is possible to live a life of integrity and purity in relationships. They can show that the true source of all love is God Himself, and that nothing that is created can take His place.

One crucial thing for someone who is discipling another person in this area is to recognise that a change of lifestyle is a loss. The prostitute has to learn to adjust to the new way of living, and may make mistakes along the way. There will be temptation to return to the old way of life, and feelings of intense frustration and pain. This is why it is important that discipling takes place within the church setting, with a supportive group of people who can understand the difficulties and support the person through the hard times, and pick them up when they fall. As Andy Comiskey says,

'Healing must be walked out in the local church. God's plan for each struggler includes becoming a dynamic part of God's solution to a broken faithless world – Christ's body, the church.'[1]

Patient and loving discipleship will enable new believers to learn from their mistakes, to see that sexual relationships will not meet the deepest need of acceptance and love, and to learn about the gracious and ever-forgiving love of God. As damaged individuals learn to love themselves, the distorted view of love will be healed. Gradually they will learn that inner peace comes from serving God, and that there is no freedom in slavishly following every instinct.

Maturity and healing are gradual processes, the renewal of minds a continuous process. The individual will learn to hate sin because God hates it. And as the woman grows within the church she will see that others also struggle with their sexuality, that single heterosexuals are called to celibacy too, that the ideal of celibacy outside marriage applies to heterosexuals as well as homosexuals, and that some find this more difficult than others.

7.3   Gender confusion

Transvestites

A transvestite is a male heterosexual who relieves emotional pressure and sexual frustration through cross-dressing, ie wearing women's clothing. Transvestites have no desire to be attractive to other men. Most men who indulge in cross-dressing have had a sense of being trapped during their childhood, a feeling of being unable to escape from their circumstances. They may have perceived themselves as second best because they are male rather than female. These thoughts may be the result of words spoken by their parents.

Transsexuals

Transsexuals (quite different from transvestites) have a deep desire to change their gender or have already done so by means of surgery and hormone treatment. Such people suffer from gender confusion (dysphoria) in a way in which transvestites do not. Unable to accept their bodies, they are convinced that they should in fact be a member of the opposite sex. Transsexuals experience a compulsion to live, behave and dress as a member of the opposite sex. They may decide to have extended hormonal treatment and

---

[1] See the recommended reading list for information on Andy Comiskey's book *Pursuing Sexual Wholeness*.

eventually surgery to change their physical bodies from male to female or vice versa.

Transsexuals tend to be lonely and isolated individuals. They are often filled with self-loathing and are deeply unhappy. Male transsexuals are not accepted in the homosexual community because they want to be women – the homosexual male has no wish to be a woman, or to have a sexual relationship with one. They also tend to be very violent towards one another because of the high level of frustration which they feel towards themselves and their lives. They may be jealous of their female friends who have periods and can become pregnant. Hormone treatment tends to lead to poor physical health in the long term. In the UK, the changing of birth certificates is illegal, and so they may never become fully accepted in their new identity. Many (though by no means all) go on to regret the step they took in having the operation done, finding that despite physical change, they have not changed in themselves, that the old hurts still exist, and that the peace they long for still eludes them.

Pointers for ministry

Working with transvestites and transsexuals is a specialised ministry, and we advise that you seek the help of people who have expertise in this. One such specialised ministry organisation in the UK is Parakaleo Ministry,[2] which has produced booklets to help people understand the particular problems in this area.

It is important for those who minister in this area not to focus on the question of gender. The real issue is the anger, bitterness and insecurity and the deep pain which they feel. Since they have in fact rejected themselves, it is important for them to understand that they are not rejected by God, and that Jesus understands their pain. It is crucial too for them to see that they are not rejected by Christians and to have the love of God affirmed in their lives, while still hearing the truth about what it means to be made in the image of God.

Gender confusion is the result of the Fall; it is the result of sin, although not necessarily the sin of the individual who is affected. According to Keith Tiller of Parakaleo, the phenomenon may be owing to sins committed against the person so affected, such as too much bonding with the opposite sex parent. Whatever the cause, Tiller says that the key to all these confusions is the deception involved, pretending to be something you are not. It is the intent to deceive which is wrong. That which is hidden needs to be brought into the light.

---

[2] Parakaleo Ministry, Box 115, Bromley, Kent, BR1 2ZA. Tel: 01782 720994. E-mail: parakaleo@btinternet.com Website: www.parakaleo.co.uk

CHAPTER 8

Addiction

'... drunkards and gluttons become poor,
and drowsiness clothes them in rags.'

(Proverbs 23:21)

Many sex workers' lives are affected, if not controlled, by drugs or alcohol. In some cases, women work to finance a drug habit, whether it is their own or their boyfriend's. Others become addicts as a result of working, perhaps because of the influence of people around them, or as a way to help them cope with their promiscuous lifestyle. Drugs and alcohol are always obtainable and may be the only thing which dulls the pain and enables them to feel that they can get through life. In this chapter, we will offer some general information about the nature of addiction problems. At the end of the chapter we will emphasise that prostitution itself can be an addiction which is as difficult to give up as any substance.

Many agencies around the country provide excellent training on drugs – the different types and their effects – as well as giving guidance on how to help people with addiction problems. Information about local courses and programmes can be obtained from social work departments and local drug agencies. Do find out what is available and make use of their expertise as part of your team's continuing training. Attending courses and seminars is also a good way to meet others who are involved in outreach of various kinds.

8.1 What is addiction?

The consumption of alcohol is legally sanctioned in this country and in other Westernised societies. In general, people drink for social reasons. Alcohol is used as a means of relaxation, to help people to talk and to help break down social barriers. However, alcohol can only do this if it is used in moderation. Alcoholism begins when the individual starts to believe that he or she cannot function or relax without a drink. Eventually, alcohol becomes the controlling factor in the person's life, often at the expense of family, marriage and employment.

Where drugs are concerned, it is important to distinguish between drug-dependence and drug misuse. Some people may only experiment with drugs occasionally, both with other people or alone. For example, they may smoke cannabis or occasionally take ecstasy or LSD, but do not become addicted. Because drugs of this sort are illegal in the UK this is known as drug misuse. Others may misuse the drugs which they receive from their GP, using painkillers, for example, to bring about a change in their mood. People who misuse drugs risk overdose and, as with alcohol use, there is always the possibility that occasional use will become habitual and thus become an addiction. Similar to an alcoholic who cannot live without a drink, a person who is drug-dependent believes that it is impossible to function without the drug, or that life is unbearable without the 'release' that the drug gives them.

People who are drug-dependent often (although not always) belong to a drug subculture. That is, they are part of a group of people whose lives revolve around drugs, who are constantly thinking about how they can get the next fix, who steal to get the money to buy drugs, and become increasingly involved in crime.

Alcoholics and drug-dependent people quickly find that life without the drug is intolerable and too painful. The psychologist Mary McMurran describes addiction as follows:

> 'A degree of involvement in a behaviour that can function to produce both pleasure and provide relief from discomfort, to the point where the cost outweighs the benefits.'[1]

In other words, what begins as a social activity, as a way to relax and enjoy oneself, becomes tyrannical, ruling the person's life. At first, there may be great social reward in drinking or taking drugs, meeting to relax or sharing the high experience. The euphoria which the drug induces is so rewarding that the person experiences an overwhelming desire to experience it again. However, drugs become tyrannical because the more the addict escapes from reality, the more the rest of life becomes out of control.

As use of the substance is continued, increasing amounts are needed to achieve the state in which the world and life looks okay again. Of course, this demands more and more money. But escalating intake also has a physical effect. At some stage, as the body becomes more dependent on a regular intake of a given substance, the addict will begin drinking or fixing to relieve the symptoms of withdrawal, which can be profoundly unpleasant and frightening.

Addicts learn to anticipate when withdrawal symptoms might step in and to time when to take the next dose in order to avoid any withdrawal whatsoever. For example, an alcoholic may take frequent drinks throughout the day to ensure that the symptoms of withdrawal do not emerge. Heavily dependent alcoholics might leave enough in the bottle to relieve the symptoms of withdrawal which they know will occur in the morning.

Unfortunately, the more the person drinks or fixes to feel 'normal', the less in touch with reality they are likely to become, and the less able they are to take responsibility for themselves. They begin to lose their dignity and self-respect: family, friends, health, employment, integrity – all these become secondary to the need to find the next drink or fix. Addicts are often the last to realise or admit that those closest to them are suffering because of their actions, and that relationships have become strained to breaking point.

What is addiction? Should we regard it as a disease, whose symptoms and consequences can be treated? Many people think so. This is the view taken by Alcoholics Anonymous, an organisation which undoubtedly has had a great deal of success in helping people to live free of alcohol and so live normal lives. Others believe there may be a genetic or inherited component of addiction. They argue that some people are born with a tendency to become addicted, and that the problem runs in families. A third view, and

---

[1] Mary McMurran's book, *The Psychology of Addiction*, is included in the recommended further reading list.

one which many psychologists take, is to see addiction as a learned behaviour which people have taken on to help them get through the pain of life, but whose use has got out of control.

Contrary to what many people think, the Bible does not say that people should not drink alcohol. As is well known, Jesus provided wine at weddings (John 2:1–11). The Bible does, however, have a good deal to say about drinking in excess, acknowledging that too much alcohol can cause financial, emotional and moral ruin. Proverbs 23:29–35 contains a remarkably graphic and accurate description of the effects of an alcoholic binge and the subsequent withdrawal symptoms.

> 'Who has woe, who has sorrow?
>   Who has strife? Who has complaints?
>   Who has needless bruises? Who has bloodshot eyes?
> Those who linger over wine,
>   who go to sample bowls of mixed wine.
> Do not gaze at wine when it is red,
>   when it sparkles in the cup,
>   when it goes down smoothly!
> In the end it bites like a snake
>   and poisons like a viper.
> Your eyes will see strange sights
>   and your mind imagine confusing things.
> You will be like one sleeping on the high seas,
>   lying on top of the rigging.
> "They hit me," you will say, "but I'm not hurt!
>   They beat me, but I don't feel it!
> When will I wake up
>   so I can find another drink?"'   (Proverbs 23:29–35)

Perhaps the best way for us to understand the Bible's approach is to see that what was intended for good and for our enjoyment has been perverted by the Fall, and like many other things, can be, and is, misused. As far as drugs are concerned, although the question is not directly tackled in the Bible, we can be guided by the fact that both the Old and New Testaments are clear that it is best for men and women to be in their right minds and sober.

8.2 Drug abuse

Within street culture, the word 'junkie' is often used to describe a drug addict. This has probably come about because of the use of the word 'junk' for drugs, but its implication that the user is also junk only adds to the feelings of self-loathing which most addicts experience. The fact is that no-one is junk; everyone is made in the image of God, and one of the women's greatest needs is to have their lack of self-respect restored and healed in Christ.

Yet there is a camaraderie among addicts, just as there is among the women who work on the streets. They share a common experience, know each others' needs (even if they are unable to help and the concern is owing to a misplaced loyalty) and meet together to alleviate the loneliness of self-obsession. Addicts often score together (ie take drugs together) for company, for safety, or out of a fear of overdosing. They may even help each other to take the drug. For example, sometimes it can be physically painful to inject, because of vein damage brought about by prolonged use. Often in these cases, a fellow user will help to inject the drug. It is also not unknown for some users to have a fear of needles and to pay someone else to inject them on a regular basis.

There are many health problems associated with drug abuse. Risks arise from impure heroin which has been contaminated by substances in order to make it go further, eg bicarbonate of soda. This can cause damage to the liver and to the veins. And of course, there is always the risk of overdose or liver damage from excessive use of prescription drugs.

However, most drug addicts are unhealthy because of self-neglect. As the addiction takes hold, more and more money is needed to pay for the drug, and so less is spent on food. The person becomes unconcerned about eating healthily (she will generally eat sweet things because drugs deplete her sugar level), as she becomes increasingly preoccupied with avoiding withdrawal from drugs. The need for instant gratification which drug-taking encourages will also mean that she is less able to have the patience to prepare and eat sensible meals.

Health problems also arise from sharing needles. It is now well known that sharing dirty needles is often responsible for the spread of the AIDS virus. Dirty needles can introduce other infections, such as pneumonia, and cause septicaemia (a poisoning of the blood) and abscesses at the injection site. In order to try to minimise these risks, many health authorities have set up needle exchanges in which clean hypodermic syringes may be obtained in exchange for used ones.

Prolonged intravenous drug use can also cause deep venous thrombosis (a clot in the vein which can prove fatal) or can lead to the veins becoming so punctured that they collapse. This means that the woman has to resort to ever more dangerous ways of injecting the drug. At first she may only use the veins in her arms, but as use becomes prolonged, she may have to start using other veins, for example, in the groin.

Drugs anaesthetise: they take away the ability to feel pain. However, emotional pain is also dulled. A person who has been numbing emotional pain in this way cannot feel grief or disappointment to the same extent as those who do not take drugs. (By the same token, an individual does not experience joy or happiness and other positive emotions.) Physical illness can remain undetected for much longer if the person is unable to feel pain. Unfortunately, however, if this sort of behaviour is prolonged, the person becomes increasingly less able to tolerate pain of any sort, whether physical or emotional. As use of the drug increases, the stresses and strains of everyday life become less tolerable. The inability to cope with any kind of pain leads to the inability to grow emotionally: a woman who has started abusing drugs at the age of 18 may not mature beyond that age until she gives them up; she will deal with hurt and stress in the same way as she would have at that age, even though she is now ten years older. A major part of rehabilitation must therefore be learning how to grow into emotional adulthood.

8.3   Alcoholism

As in all addictions, the main reason for abusing alcohol is to induce a state of being able to cope with or even avoid the difficulties of life. In severe alcoholism, the addict drinks to achieve a state of oblivion. However, instead of making life better, the prolonged and unhealthy use of alcohol only brings more problems. As in drug abuse, the risks associated with alcoholism include physical, psychological and social damage. Physically, the alcoholic runs the risk (among other things) of cirrhosis of the liver, liver and oesophageal cancer, stomach ulcers, malnutrition, stroke, heart disease and even nerve and brain damage. It is well known that excessive use of alcohol during pregnancy can damage the unborn child.

Psychologically, excessive drinking can cause blackouts, in which the individual cannot remember events which took place during a binge. On the other hand there may be selective memory, in which the alcoholic remembers only the good parts of an event, but fails to recall the bad behaviour which caused the event to be spoiled for everyone present. This is known as euphoric recall.

This kind of behaviour, in turn, leads to the breakdown of relationships as the alcoholic becomes preoccupied with finding the next drink and less tolerant of those who object to overbearing and selfish behaviour. Many crimes are committed by people who are under the influence of alcohol, and violence is common. As the difficulties increase, the addict places herself outside reality, and an impenetrable wall is built around the real state of the emotions – this is what prevents the alcoholic from seeing that she is destroying herself.

8.4   Prostitution as an addiction

It is quite possible for a woman to be addicted to a combination of substances, eg alcohol, cocaine and valium. When ministering to someone who is addicted to both alcohol and drugs it is important to discern which addiction is the strongest, ie which one has the strongest hold over her life.

Circumstances may dictate that they consume more alcohol than drugs, but the drugs may be the stronger addiction. A way to discern which addiction is stronger is to see which one is more effective in blotting out the pain and helping them to forget their situation. Often, drug-users have difficulty admitting that they are alcoholics as well.

When the word 'addiction' is mentioned, most people think of drugs or alcohol. However, we want to emphasise that prostitution itself can be an addiction, which can prove to be as hard to give up as alcohol or drugs. Women who work on the streets become dependent not only on the income, but on the prostitution community itself. While there is ultimately very little loyalty, there is a camaraderie to be found on the beat, and the women often find a sense of belonging and acceptance on the streets which they may not be able to find anywhere else.

The work itself gives some identity: it is a job – something which has to be done in order to stay alive; in the short-term at least, it gives a reason for living. Not only that, there may be some comfort from the physical closeness (however short-lived) which prostitution entails, and an adrenaline buzz from the continual sense of danger and excitement. Thus, while a woman may admit that her life is miserable, she may be reluctant to change because it is what she knows. Sometimes, women who have had the opportunity to begin a lifestyle away from prostitution have found that they cannot stop working. They long for the excitement of working, for the companionship, and for the sense of identity it gives them. They may feel that their services are needed (perhaps by a regular customer), and thus convince themselves that they are wanted and valued. They may keep returning to the work, because to leave it constitutes a loss which is hard to bear. Furthermore, they may have difficulty in admitting that prostitution is an addiction and a problem, since this adds to the list of reasons for lacking self-respect. Praise God, that Jesus can give them hope: let's ensure they hear about it.

> *'For my Father's will is that everyone who looks to the Son and believes in him shall have eternal life, and I will raise him up at the last day.'*   (John 6:40)

Case study

Addiction and consequences

Katie is 23 years old. Her parents were both alcoholic and at two years of age she was taken into a foster home. Her sisters were put into a children's home. When she was ten, she was given lager to drink by her foster father. Katie ran away from home when she was 15 and lived on the streets. For a few years she was in and out of prison on charges of breach of the peace, but managed to stay out of prostitution and away from drugs. However, when she was 21 she moved to another city and started to work on the streets. Then she became pregnant. During her pregnancy Katie was drinking heavily, but after her baby was born, she stopped drinking completely and devoted herself to looking after her little girl. However, when the baby was one year old, Katie started drinking again and the child was taken away from her by social services. Katie tried hard to stay off alcohol, and even went into a rehab, but she found it too difficult and ran away. Now her sister is looking after her daughter, and Katie is back on the streets and drinking heavily. Katie has never touched drugs.

CHAPTER 9

Rehabilitation

*'Seek first his kingdom and his righteousness,
and all these things will be given to you as well.'*

(Matthew 6:33)

9.1   Ministering to the addict

Your first priority in reaching out to those with addiction problems is not that they should stop using drugs or alcohol; it is to communicate the love of Jesus. He Himself had a reputation for being a glutton and a drunkard – this suggests that He did not demand that those He ministered to give up their habits. Rather, He demanded belief in who He was, and change followed on from this.

As you get to know a woman and continue to show her His love, He will work the transformation in her, and she will begin to want to change. This will include wanting to be rid of the addiction. God does not work to a prescribed formulae when He intervenes in people's lives. Some Christians do have a gift which enables them to minister in God's power and see people miraculously freed from the power of addiction. This not only makes the addict easier to deal with, but is also a powerful form of evangelism to others. There is no doubt that God can and does work in power in some people's lives and cause miraculous changes in their lifestyles and habits. When Jesus called the 12 disciples, He gave them authority to drive out demons and cure diseases, sending them out to preach the kingdom of God and heal the sick (Matthew 9:1ff). If worship is the prime motivation for our ministry, we may well see God act through us in this way. However, it is important not to expect God to work in any particular way, or try to force healing. If God gives you a gift in this area, then praise Him. If He does not, He is surely working in other ways!

Most people with addiction problems, however, have to go through the trauma of withdrawal and detoxification. In the case of drug addicts, this usually means that they will suffer severe flu-like symptoms for a few days. An alcoholic may well need immediate medical and nursing care if she stops drinking abruptly, and will most likely need medication to help her through the initial stages of withdrawal.

Physical withdrawal from drugs and alcohol, however, is only part of the story. If a person has been escaping from life for many years and wreaking havoc in her own and others' lives, a great deal of work needs to be done to repair relationships and to help the addict to come out of a failed mindset. What do we mean by this?

People with addiction problems need to learn to be honest with themselves and others, to recognise when they are rationalising (ie making excuses for their behaviour), to stop blaming others for what has happened and to learn to take full responsibility for their actions. They need to learn not to project their self-hatred on to other people, and to be realistic about their and others' limitations. They need to learn to cope with the crippling guilt which can so easily trigger a return to addictive behaviour. In other words, they need to have a thorough understanding and appreciation of the need for forgiveness.

This is where Christian teaching comes in: only Jesus can give us an appropriate sense of our identity. We can receive our healing from Jesus, bringing each addiction to the foot of the cross. Such a renewal of the mind needs careful nurturing and guiding on the part of caring workers who understand the damage that addiction can cause and are willing to disciple and patiently love as the individual recovers. For most, a place at a Christian rehabilitation centre will help in this process of growing in the Lord and gradual release from the power of addiction.

'If the Son sets you free, you will be free indeed.'   (John 8:36)

9.2   Rehabilitation centres

As we have already seen, some people who come off drugs don't need rehabilitation, but most do. In the first place, it is unrealistic to expect long-term change while the woman stays in the same environment in which the problems arise and persist. It is usually best for her to be removed from a peer group which encourages her to continue taking drugs or alcohol, if her family circumstances permit this. Although she derives her identity from this group at present, it is ultimately a destructive force in her life.

Many secular agencies provide opportunities for women with drug and alcohol addictions to try to give up their drug habit. The Health Services reserve places in psychiatric units for detoxification. That is, they provide a safe environment in which users may discontinue their drug abuse under medical supervision. Social work departments and voluntary organisations (Christian and secular) also provide support for those who want to give up drugs. They run residential units which offer structured rehabilitation programmes for those who have already undergone withdrawal from drugs. Most rehabilitation units adopt the 12-Step programme which has been devised by Alcoholics Anonymous. In this the addict acknowledges that life has got out of control and that they have become powerless in the face of their addiction. Only then can recovery take place.

Some rehabilitation centres take on both alcohol and drug abusers, but in the main, units are specialised and experienced in one area or the other. Even if an addict is drug-free there is still a need to unlearn the wrong mental habits which have dominated life. There is a need to learn how to handle stress and remain drug-free. To be drug-free means to be free of a craving for drugs, and of the longing to escape the reality of life. This can take many years of recovery even after a person has become physically clean.

9.3   Choosing a rehabilitation centre

If a woman requests to go to a rehabilitation centre, try to find out why she wants to go. Ask her what she thinks her needs are and what she expects from rehabilitation. This may be very different from your own thinking on the matter! It may be that she wants to avoid people on the street, or escape a custodial sentence. It may even be that she wants to have a comfortable place to stay for a while. If this is the case, success is less likely, although not impossible.

Some women find it very difficult to know their own desires, let alone articulate them. The consolation is that earnest prayer can reveal the truth, and help distinguish the 'sheep from the goats' – those who genuinely want help and those who have ulterior motives. Whatever the case, it is important to support the woman if she expresses a desire to change, and to help her on the first step to achieving her goal. She is looking for a kind of promised land, a place in which she is free from her oppressors – Satan, drugs, and those who supply those drugs – and she will need help. However, rehabilitation should never be seen as the whole answer to a person's problems. It is very important to communicate this – that going to a rehabilitation centre is only the beginning of making the right choices which will lead to true freedom.

People who are involved in the drug scene are often subject to strong peer-group pressure which they find difficult to withstand because they lack a sense of personal identity. If the woman lives in a major city, try to find a rehabilitation centre as far away from it as possible. If she is 300 miles away from her drug environment, it takes some determination to return. If she is in the same city, it is only a bus ride away.

Workers have an added complication to their chemical addiction: their damaged sense of themselves and a distorted view of sexuality. It is therefore vital that the rehabilitation unit has staff members with expertise in sexual counselling. Where a girl or rent boy has exhibited sexual confusion (homosexual tendencies), a mixed rehabilitation centre is often best. It can be quite a daunting prospect for a homosexual to go into an all-male rehabilitation centre in which most of the residents are heterosexual. For some, such a prospect will have strong associations with prison.

9.4   The application process

Applying for a place at a rehabilitation centre is a lengthy and frustrating process. It is lengthy because it takes a great many letters and phone calls to secure a place and arrange a time for admission, and frustrating because there may be delays; it may be difficult to find an appropriate centre, or funding for the place could take a long time to come through. The exceptions to this may be applications to Christian agencies, such as Teen Challenge, which do not rely on DSS funding for their work.

At present in the UK, a social services approved community care assessor must assess all applications for financial support for residential services. The assessor is usually a social worker, a drug or alcohol worker from a specialist agency, or a probation officer. Each area has its own procedures and systems, and the law changes from time to time. Your local drug/alcohol agency or the chosen rehabilitation centre will help you to find out who to contact. The community care officer will help in the application and coordinate the funding. Here is a list of people you will have to liaise with if you are helping a woman apply to a rehabilitation centre:

- her GP

- her social worker

- the DSS (or equivalent) for funding the place

- her family

- her psychiatrist

- the person in charge of the unit

- her probation officer

Maintaining clear communication with other agencies, including the rehabilitation centre, is essential. So is regular updating of information on matters such as costs, the availability of funding and possible date of admission. Let the woman know that you are liaising with the statutory bodies involved in rehabilitation, eg social services, probation.

The prospect of going through an unmasking experience is terrifying. It is therefore essential to explain to the woman the details of the unit's programme before she gets there. Ask the rehabilitation centre for the relevant information. For example, the length of stay in a unit can vary from three months to two years, depending on an individual's needs and/or the programme run by the unit. The woman will probably have to sign a contract, which may include an agreement not to leave the premises unaccompanied for the first few weeks. Practical information about things such as bathroom facilities, the possibility of room sharing, and what toiletries and clothing she will need to take, is vital. Make sure she has all this information in writing so that she can refer to it as often as she wants.

Sometimes it is appropriate to go on a visit with the woman before she is admitted. For some it is better to go to the unit without having seen it first, striking while the iron is hot and seizing the opportunity for her to go for rehabilitation while she is willing. She might very quickly change her mind, because she is afraid of the change which attending a rehabilitation centre might involve.

Be understanding. For the client, it is a very big step to go into a rehabilitation centre. Fear tends to cripple risk-taking, even if it is a good risk. The prospect of facing life's hurts without painkillers can prove too daunting for many addicts. There could be fear of failure, of letting the family down (again), fear of losing the 'security' of drug-taking and working on the streets. Some women fear that going into a rehabilitation centre will cut them off from people who understand them and accept them. There might also be fear of becoming institutionalised, especially if the woman has a background of being in children's homes or prison. It is also possible to be afraid of success, afraid that they will be unable to sustain doing well, because failure is what they are used to and are comfortable with.

Once the woman has been accepted by the rehabilitation centre, it is important that the person who has built up a relationship with her continues to support her during her stay. This can be done by sending cards and letters, phoning and visiting, and praying with and for her. She may not be allowed visitors or be allowed to leave the unit unaccompanied by a member of staff for the first two weeks. It is useful for you to know the rules of the house so that you can support her in sticking to the terms of the contract which she will have to sign when she is first admitted.

9.5 Life after rehabilitation – discipling and follow-up

All addicts find rehabilitation programmes difficult. Not only do they have to discover how to be drug-free, they also have to learn to face the future without drugs, change their thinking habits and plan for a life without previous friends and accomplices. While some people do last the course, some will be unable to tolerate the programme, and its enclosed communal way of living which most rehabilitation centres entail. Some people who leave rehabilitation centres before completing the programme have been known to say, 'It is so hard to handle love.' Those who work with addicts have to come to terms with the fact that the women may often have been to many rehabilitation centres and been through several programmes. They may even have so much experience of rehabilitation centres that they know the jargon and the process but are able to remain aloof from it, returning to old ways when they leave the units. This is par for the course, and it is important that you stick by the woman and not be overwhelmed by disappointment.

By the same token, it is possible for someone to complete a rehabilitation programme successfully only to return home and discover a need to replace the excitement of drugs with that of working on the streets again. Very soon a drug habit resurfaces to deaden the pain which accompanies the guilt of working. Alternatively, a person who has learned to channel life's pains through 'non-respectable' and addictive behaviour may well adopt another 'respectable' addiction, such as workaholism, without dealing with the pain.

This is why it is important for recovering addicts to be discipled in a church setting. Recovery is slow and not easy; but a loving church group can provide the support which gives the woman the encouragement to persevere. It is crucial for women to see that the church itself, because it is made up of people, is not perfect, but that it can be a nurturing and loving place.

> *'We who are strong ought to bear with the failings of the weak and not please ourselves.'* (Romans 15:1)

Many women have financial debts as a result of their addiction. They will need money to live on and for housing. Most will be entitled to benefits from social security. Equally, most will know exactly what benefits they are entitled to. If they do not, you can help them to find out. The best source of information is the welfare rights officer in any social work area. Most rehabilitation centres will help to teach the woman how to budget and pay bills and so on, but she may need continued help with this once she leaves the centre. If she has long-standing bills (electricity, gas and so on) or outstanding court fines it may be possible for her to pay them off weekly over a period of time. She may also have debts to drug dealers and friends. Do try, however, to resist the temptation to bail her out of past financial difficulties which continue to cause problems in the present. It is important for her to make mistakes and learn to recover from them herself. If someone else always takes care of her finances, she will never learn to take responsibility for them herself. Sometimes this kind of tough love is necessary in order to help a woman to learn how to take care of herself. Bearing one another's burdens may mean allowing someone to make mistakes.

Sometimes you may have to help women find accommodation. This may mean anything from a hostel for the homeless or temporary care home, to her own house. It is best, if possible, to work with social services to achieve this, because they have access to resources you may not have. They may also be able to help with applications for housing benefits. You may find that you have to send a referral letter to a council housing office or housing association to support the person's application. (For an example of a referral letter, see page 109.) When you write these letters it is important to emphasise the risks which are involved in leaving this person without accommodation. Housing authorities may wish to know where they have been living before, whether the person is or has been a victim of domestic violence, whether they are HIV-positive, and their current housing status. Other information which may be of use is whether they have a methadone prescription, if they are on sickness benefit, or if they have children. These factors add up and are reconsidered as part of a points system. The more points a woman has, the more likely she is to be given accommodation.

> *'I have come that they may have life, and have it to the full.'* (John 10:10)

CHAPTER 10

Your team and other agencies

'If it is possible, as far as it depends on you, live at peace with everyone.'

(Romans 12:18)

10.1   Liaising with other agencies

In the UK there are two types of organisations which may be involved in caring for sex workers. Statutory bodies are organisations funded by the government, eg housing authorities, the health authority or the social work department. Voluntary organisations are groups who are not answerable to the state but who work within their own ideals and have been set up independently of the government's provision for groups and individuals within society.

As you build up your ministry it will be necessary for you to liaise with these other agencies. For example, if you are involved in helping someone to find a place in a rehabilitation unit, you will have to work with social services, and probably also with health workers and housing authorities. It is important that we are seen to have integrity and to work to high standards. In this way we will gain the respect of outsiders (1 Thessalonians 4:12). In this chapter we will give you some tips for working alongside voluntary organisations and statutory bodies. The way in which you go about this can be a method of evangelism for those who work in these organisations.

From both the client's point of view and that of statutory bodies, it is important that you should not be seen as working in isolation, as though you alone have the solution to the problems facing the women. Be open about all that you do, and be willing to learn from other people. At least make a point of finding out which statutory bodies are involved in the care of the women you are working with.

You are a non-statutory organisation, and you are not accountable to statutory bodies unless you have gained funding from them. Consider your liaising with the statutory bodies as consulting with those who can help your client recover from her addiction and way of life. It is important to be open with these agencies about the client's background, eg how long she has worked, her criminal record and so on. Make sure she knows your confidentiality policy and understands why the sharing of information is necessary before any information is divulged.

Your intervention should not be at odds with that of other organisations. If there is a statutory body, try to become a part of the multidisciplinary team which works for the woman's welfare. This will probably be headed up by a psychiatrist or perhaps by a social worker. If you become involved in case conferences or are part of a multi-disciplinary team set-up, let the statutory body call the tune. For example, the probation officer, knowing that the woman sees you more often than her, may ask you for a regular report. Remember, though, to ask her permission before you agree to do this.

Always remember that these organisations are under no obligation to work with you, to answer your questions or to give you information. We have to work to gain their respect, show that we are trustworthy, that we work with due respect for confidentiality, and that we have the woman's best interests, rather than our own political or spiritual agenda, at heart. If you are careless in your work and are unreliable, or overstep the mark and do work which you are not entitled by law to do (such as arrange a place in a rehabilitation unit without having arranged finance first), then you will quite justifiably incur the displeasure of these agencies and will not be included in their work with the women.

Always show the woman respect by asking her permission before speaking for her or acting on her behalf.

It is important to show the women that you can work as part of a team and lovingly accept groups with a different outlook from yourselves. This is especially important among groups within Christendom. If you hear the women comment on the negative attitude between two Christian groups (eg 'you don't like each other, do you?'), you should think carefully about your attitude towards other outreach organisations.

10.2   Social services case conferences

Social services hearings are set up to assess a course of action or decide a format to monitor the client's progress (or lack of it). The hearings may include social workers, GPs, police, psychiatrists, probation officers, outreach workers, nursery nurses, and relatives. The size of the meeting may vary from nine to 15, and the social worker in charge of the case decides who should attend.

If you are asked to attend a social work case conference, inform the woman of the invitation. Check with her if she is willing to attend, and make sure she is happy for you to do so. It is crucial that she knows what information you are likely to share, and for you to have her permission to do so. Only thus can you build up trust.

It may be that it is enough for you to provide a written monthly report for the social worker on your relationship with the woman and how you feel she is getting on. The advantage of this is that you are less likely to be seen as another authority figure. The report will be most beneficial if it contains a balance of both negative and positive aspects of the woman's life and behaviour.

10.3   Police custody

Crime is part and parcel of prostitution. Most workers have a police record which could include anything from soliciting to robbery, drug dealing, credit card frauds, theft and even manslaughter. As you work with the women, it is quite likely that you will be involved in helping those who have been arrested.

The length of police custody – the result of an arrest – may range from a few hours' detention to an overnight stay in the police station awaiting a court hearing the following day. The length of custody is determined by the time of arrest, the woman's criminal records and the behaviour of the person under arrest. The maximum length of time a person may be held in a police station is 72 hours. Always check that the woman has legal representation. Most solicitors have emergency numbers, which means that they can be contacted outside normal office hours. Check that the woman is in possession of this number at all times. You will not always be around to help her. It is important to cultivate some sort of independence in the woman and for her to begin to take responsibility for her own actions.

People can feel very lonely and vulnerable in prison. It is crucial that you take the presence of Jesus to her. Remember what Jesus said (Matthew 25:36): *'I was in prison and you came to visit me.'* As a member of a non-statutory organisation you are there as her friend, someone who is supporting her in the absence of, or in addition to, her family. Carry your identity card with you at all times. It is at the station sergeant's discretion whether you will be admitted to see the woman or not. Evidence of your identity and what you stand for will help you see her more speedily. If you are unable to see her, think about sending her a note with some Scripture verses in it. You may even be able to hand in clothes and cigarettes.

10.4   Court appearances

'God disciplines us for our good, that we may share in his holiness.'
(Hebrews 12:10)

Accompanying the woman to the court is a great opportunity for you to show the love of Jesus. The level of support you give, however, should be proportionate to her desire to change and get out of the lifestyle, and to what you feel God is telling you to do.

If possible arrange to meet her before the hearing. This is a good opportunity to pray with her. No matter how indifferent she is to her personal salvation, it is unlikely that she will refuse prayer at this point in her life.

If possible, try to arrange to meet her at her home, and to accompany her to the court. It is always possible that she will panic at the last minute and run away, thus failing to attend the hearing. Allow plenty of time between your arrival at the woman's home and the appointment at the court.

It is common for a worker to have four or five outstanding cases at any given time. It is also common for a worker to have two or three different names in operation at one time, ie to be required to appear in court under several different identities, and to have several different legal transactions taking place simultaneously. If a person fails to attend court, a warrant for arrest is issued that same day. The best thing they can do in that situation is go to a police station and turn themselves in immediately.

Court reports

You may find that you are required to write a court report for the woman. Remember that magistrates and judges assess the professionalism of an organisation by the quality of its written reports. The authorities do realise that your work is voluntary, and this will carry weight. Your report could greatly help a woman's case or greatly hinder it. If you are required to attend court, remember to be smartly dressed and to encourage the woman to be so, too. Remember, if you are involved in a court case at all liaise with the woman's solicitor. Here are some guidelines for writing reports:

- A court report should include certain factual details, but you should be guided by the solicitor. The emphasis given in the report will depend on the nature of the court appearance.

  The following should be included:
  - how long you have known the woman
  - how long your organisation has known her, and in what capacity
  - note improvements which have taken place in her lifestyle since you have known her
  - outline her accommodation and financial situation
  - suggest solutions to prevent re-offending
  - give the names of other organisations involved and with whom you are liaising

  Four copies of a court report are required
  - one for the ruling body
  - one for the solicitor
  - one for the worker
  - one for your own records

- Always keeps a copy even after the court case is over as this is an important reference for you and your colleagues.

- It is important not to suggest solutions which are not practically possible. For example it is a criminal offence to offer a place in a rehabilitation centre when funding is not yet available. Quite apart from this, the court would regard this as deceitful and unrighteous.

- Confidentiality is of the utmost importance. Christian support in a legal crisis, if it is handled correctly, can promote trust, a trust which is rarely found in legal circles. It can give a glimpse of how much Jesus loves those involved.

■ Friends, family or non-statutory organisations can stand assurity for a defendant. This means that you provide bail to prevent the woman from going to prison. It means that you guarantee that the woman will behave in a certain way. For example you may be required to give assurance that she will attend for the next court case; go to the police station at a fixed time each week; not re-offend while on bail; and so on. It means that if the woman fails to behave in the way she says she will, you will be required to pay a sum of money agreed by the judge or sheriff or magistrate. No money is exchanged between the courts and the people who stand assurity if the client behaves in the way required by the court. Evidence of your financial status will often be required at court to assess your suitability in standing assurity. For example, you may be required to provide a bank statement and/or a building society account. The amount required by the court (normally between £100 and £300) will depend on factors such as the seriousness of previous convictions, outstanding matters still to come to court, and the alleged criminal offence.

If you do this, and the woman's behaviour before the court appearance causes you to regret your action you should go to the local police station and rescind on the assurity. In other words, declare that you are no longer willing to stand the bail for the defendant. A warrant will then automatically be sent out for her arrest. You should tell the woman concerned what you intend to do and ensure that she understands why you are doing it.

10.5 Prison

According to Scottish and English law, an individual is innocent until proven guilty. In theory, this should mean that no-one is held against their will unless they have been sentenced by a court of law. Nevertheless, the remand system can hold a person for three to 18 months before he or she comes to trial. Longer periods of remand are less common but not unknown. It is quite possible for people who have been held on remand for many months to have the case thrown out by the court because of lack of evidence.

Some prisoners are able to use prison to their own advantage, using the time to acquire an education, sometimes to degree level. For the majority, however, prison is known as 'crime college', and what was lacking in their criminal knowledge before their sentence will be supplied during their time in custody. Occult activity, homosexual and lesbian activity, rape, violence, drug-smuggling and drug-taking are all part of prison life. It has been known for cannabis-smoking to be tolerated in order to keep the prisoners in a passive, peaceful state, and to make life easier for overworked staff. Racism is to be found between different groupings and cultures, not merely between black and white.

Suicide, although guarded against, is relatively common, caused by frustration, isolation, and the feeling that one's voice will not be heard over and above the strength of the institution and its traditions.

Drugs of any form or shape are common in prison, despite the attempts of the authorities to stop them being smuggled in. Many prisons offer the support of Narcotics Anonymous and other drug agencies. The medical services within the prison itself may offer detox services for prisoners.

In the UK, mothers who give birth while in prison can have their babies with them for up to nine months. Those with children have their own cell and do not have to share with other prisoners. Unfortunately, this can have a detrimental effect on the child, who learns that it is normal to have the undivided attention of the mother 24 hours a day. In a sense, the child is sentenced too, and lacks the freedom and experience which characterises the lives of most infants. After nine months, if the mother has to stay in prison, she is separated from her child. When this happens, it is common for the mother to experience an overwhelming sense of powerlessness, of having nothing to love and take care of. At its worst, the sense of loss can be such that she feels she has nothing to live for. There is no quick answer to such sadness. We can only have the courage to be compassionate:

'Remember those in prison as if you were their fellow prisoners, and those who are ill-treated as if you yourselves were suffering.' (Hebrews 13:3)

Transsexuals are very vulnerable in prison. They are often segregated from other prisoners (along with the criminally insane, police informers, corrupt police, sex offenders and so on) because it is felt that they are at risk. It is difficult for a transsexual who may suddenly find himself in male clothing and in an all-male environment for the first time in years. He may be subject to ridicule from other prisoners, as well as from the prison staff. Prison officers have been known to refuse to give them razors in order to humiliate them. On the other hand, transsexuals can be very popular in prison because they are the nearest thing to a woman for many of the prisoners. Some transsexuals resort to prostitution in prison, often protected by clients who act as a kind of ponce and drug dealer. (Hormone tablets are not allowed in prison, but they can be obtained by those who know how and where to get them.)

Guidelines for visiting prisoners

'I was in prison and you came to visit me.' (Matthew 25:36)

- Remember that you are visiting prisoners on behalf of an organisation, not as a private individual. The final decision as to whether or not you may visit a prisoner rests with the governor of the prison, and the regulations are strict. Prior to your visit, send a report outlining the nature of your organisation, the aims and objectives of your visits, and

how you think you might help facilitate the inmate's recovery from
addiction or criminal behaviour.

- If possible, phone a few days in advance. A letter of introduction plus
  some form of personal identification are required. If the person is on
  remand you may undertake a general visit, which does not need to be
  booked in advance.

- In most remand prisons, a visit from a non-statutory organisation would
  have the same legal status as those of solicitors and social workers. Long-
  term prisons would classify such a visit as a probation visit.

- Each prison has its own rules regarding what items may be taken to the
  inmate. It is best to phone the prison to check what you can take.
  Inappropriate behaviour is frowned upon, and you will not normally be
  given a second chance. Passing objects to prisoners, unacceptable hugs,
  showing disrespect to prison staff, and being repeatedly late for visits,
  may disqualify you from visiting. Make sure you follow the guidelines
  for visiting provided by the prison.

- Do inform Prison Fellowship of your visit – they are very prayerful.

Sample housing reference report

Your office address: . . . .
. . . .

Housing agency address: . . . .
. . . .

Date: . . . .

Ref: . . . .

Dear Sir/Madam

Case: Annette Moore, DOB 19/6/64

I am contacting you in the capacity of community outreach worker with the
. . . .
project. This voluntary sector project works in the local area with clients in high-need
categories. It liaises with local specialist units, social services and the probation
services. The duties of the outreach worker include providing practical and emotional
support and guidance. It is in this capacity that I am involved with Annette.

I have known Annette Moore for 19 months. During this time she has been given
emotional and practical support by the project, and she has successfully stabilised
what was a chaotic lifestyle brought about by drug abuse. She keeps regular contact
with her GP in (address).

The reason for this referral is as follows. Until recently, Annette was resident at
. . . .
During her time there she became the victim of repeated physical violence. The
situation got out of control and the house was eventually boarded up by the police. As
a result of this stress Annette suffered a temporary relapse into heroin abuse. Since this
incident, Annette has had to share accommodation with other drug-users. However,
she has managed to stay drug-free for some three months. Her GP is willing to
corroborate this.

In conclusion, I recommend Annette for emergency housing for two reasons:
(a) She is constantly under threat of violence from other drug-users as long as she is
    sharing accommodation with them;
(b) She is at risk of relapse if her accommodation is not changed.

Thank you in advance for your consideration

Yours faithfully

Community outreach worker

CHAPTER 11

Spiritual matters

'For I am convinced that neither death nor life, neither angels nor demons, neither the present nor the future, nor any powers, neither height nor depth, nor anything else in all creation, will be able to separate is from the love of God that is in Christ Jesus our Lord.'

(Romans 8:38–39)

According to the Gospels, Jesus heals both mind and spirit. In Acts 10:38, it is said of Him that God anointed Him 'with the Holy Spirit and power' and that He went around doing good and healing all who were under the power of the devil 'because God was with Him'. As children of God we are called to follow Jesus' example.

Satan is particularly active in prostitution areas. However, we should not imagine that there are 'no go areas' of spiritual authority in which God's sovereignty is limited. Let's see God's love smashing strongholds in these areas. We have been given spiritual weapons to demolish strongholds which are opposed to God (2 Corinthians 10:3–5). He has given us power and authority to uncover the lies of satanic darkness in our world.

In this section we will consider two aspects of spiritual darkness – the occult, and demonic attack. We cannot wage war if we do not know who our enemy is and where he is. Essential information is required for war between nations, and it is no different in the unseen world. Further, often evil can be disguised as goodness. We must be constantly in prayer to God asking for His wisdom and discernment. If you find that you are becoming involved in this kind of ministry – don't work alone. Seek the guidance and help of a respected believer who has a particular gift in this area.

11.1   The occult

'For our struggle is not against flesh and blood, but against the rulers, against the authorities, against the powers of this dark world and against the spiritual forces of evil in the heavenly realms.'   (Ephesians 6:12)

The word 'occult' means 'hidden'. That which is not of God has to be hidden – it is part of spiritual darkness, and cannot belong to the light which God gives the world. The Bible explicitly forbids all involvement in all occultic practices including seances, witchcraft and fortune telling. Such practices are 'detestable to the Lord' (eg Leviticus 19:31; 20:6; Deuteronomy 18:10–12).

Most prostitutes have had some exposure to the occult during their childhood, whether in their families, in children's homes or other institutions such as convents. Others may have learnt about tarot cards and ouija boards in prison. Repeated involvement in occult practices may have an addictive effect as psychological habits are formed. Examples of occultic activity are:

- ouija boards
- tarot cards
- New Age movement as a disguise for witchcraft
- dungeons and dragons
- satanic crime conferences in which fantasy becomes reality

- transcendental meditation

- yoga

- white and black witches

- Satanism (includes addiction to blood and human flesh, black magic and perverted religious ritual in which drink, drugs and human flesh may be consumed and orgiastic sex performed)

- abuse ritual in which repeated physical, mental, spiritual, and emotional onslaught is combined with a systematic use of symbols and ceremonies designed to turn the victim against herself, society and God. This may include sex with children, and other kinds of abuse to bring about fear and inflict pain

Occult practices attract people who want to have power. They may want to manipulate and control others, or to cause harm to someone. For some it may be a way to boost low self-esteem. Others become involved out of a conscious desire to rebel against God, and still others become involved because they want to increase their knowledge of the supernatural. Involvement in the occult, however, can only harm the individual, and may lead to depression, chronic fear, inability to control anger, and sleeping difficulties.

There is no doubt that occultic involvement opens the way for demonic activity in a person's life. One word of caution, however. These symptoms are not necessarily indicative of occult involvement. While it is true that Satan is active in areas of prostitution, simply because he is allowed entry into people's lives to create strongholds, we must remember that not every aspect of a woman's life is to be put down to demonic activity. In other words, don't look for or imagine that there are demons lurking in every corner. It is important to recognise that people are responsible for their own actions, that certain behaviour may be attributable to foolishness, wrong decisions in life, addictions or even simply bad temper. A recognition of the spiritual element does not rule out the use of common sense.

Ministry with those who have been involved in the occult must be done very carefully. Many will have suffered from rejection in the past, so a good relationship between the counsellor and the person being ministered to is essential. The person who comes for help must really want to change, and it may mean that she has to move away from her environment and the people who are influencing her. This will help her to believe that she can be pure and free. If the woman is involved in witchcraft or organised occultic practices, find out more by asking:

- which order she is a member of

- who the priest or priestess is

- what the working names of the members of the order are

- which gods they worship.

Make a future appointment with the person and make sure you pray about the situation with your prayer partner. Remember that each individual must accept and take responsibility for her sin. The lie which the enemy tells those who are involved is that they do not need to turn away from the practices because they have been victims. At some point, however, each individual must make a personal choice as to whom she will follow. It is important, too, that she is helped to renounce her involvement in occult practices (even if she has been involved only indirectly), and to know that she is forgiven. Continue to minister to each individual through Bible study and prayer.

11.2   Deliverance from demonic attack

As we have said, dabbling in the occult is a very common way for demons to gain entry into a person's life. So too, is any form of addiction, in which the person has no control over his or her life when addiction has taken hold, and has no knowledge or control of what influences may be taking over his or her life. Similarly, those who are involved in occult activity very often have a perverse sexual life.

A general guideline for ministry is to watch out for the ruling spirit in a person's life. This could be lust, or manipulation (the 'Jezebel spirit'), homosexuality, lies, independence, pride or self-destruction, or isolation. In all our dealings with people who walk in this kind of darkness we will become aware of the demonic influence over the people's lives. We will see resistance to God, sin, blasphemy, addictions, depression and suicidal ideas. These are symptoms of lives not brought out of the darkness and under the influence of demons. Occasionally, you may come across actual manifestations, in which it becomes clear that there is a demonic spirit in control of this person's life. Such demonic possession may been caused by deliberate invitation on the part of the individual, eg by subscribing to a satanic group or beliefs.

Alternatively, it could be caused by others who have cursed the person or by mediums who have instructed the demon to go into a person. These manifestations are most likely to occur while you are praying with a person, during a counselling session, or when the demon is aware of being in the presence of someone in whom Christ dwells.

Here are some signs of demonic attack:

- a complete change in personality

- an apparent domination of the individual by an alien individuality

- rapid change of facial expression from friendliness to an dreadful black look

- sudden change of voice

- new personality with new contents of consciousness

- flailing limbs

- destructive behaviour

- violence towards those present

- physical strength even in frail people

- cursing and blasphemy against God

- expression of aversion to the Word of God

- aversion to divine things

- clairvoyance

- complete cure after expulsion

The story of the Gerasene demoniac in Mark 1:1–15 is a good illustration from Scripture as to what happens in this phenomenon. The man with the demon has great strength and is physically uncontrollable, constantly flailing about and restless. He is also very noisy and cut himself with stones. The man wants help and the demons within him know very well who Jesus is.[1]

Although evidence of demonic influence can be extremely frightening, and demons can have profound control over people's lives, the truth is that demons are overcome by the blood of the Lamb (Revelation 12:11). Satan seeks to oppose God's purpose and hinder the development of His people. God's image can be hideously distorted. However, God's power can restore that 'broken image' and we can say with confidence that 'The Lamb that was slain shall receive the rewards of his suffering.' Jesus' death is not in vain.

It is also crucial to remember that you are on the winning side. Jesus has already won the battle. Furthermore, you are not fighting the battle, you are merely acting in Jesus' name. It is Jesus who is Lord, not Satan, and not you. Jesus is the end of the demons. There is no question of defeat: the battle is already won. You are not the person who does the deliverance – it is Jesus who works through you. As Psalm 49:7 says, *'No man can redeem the life of another'* – this is exclusively the work of Christ. Liberation is possible only through Christ.

Guidelines for ministry

Never attempt deliverance prayers alone. Always work within a team. Check your impressions with a prayer partner and with the rest of the team. This is

---

[1] See Koch (1973), p. 266.

part of discernment. Someone else may be given an insight into a situation, or may have experience which can guide you. Organise prayer partners who can pray for you while you are ministering.

If you really feel that someone needs deliverance – examine your motives. Do you want a disciple of Jesus or someone who has been delivered?

Always let God dictate the pace. Satan can often make a situation appear to be an emergency. It is wise not to move towards deliverance in a climate of panic, fear or a feeling that 'it has to be now'.

It should be possible to distinguish clearly between mental illness and demonic influence. The person who is demonised will remain sane in his thoughts, i.e. we will not see evidence of hallucinations (seeing things or hearing voices which are not there) or delusions (false beliefs which are at odds with the culture in which the person is living) in the person.

The word 'deliverance' tends either to be completely scorned, feared or sensationalised. For those working in ministry with prostitutes, there is a need to recognise that there is certainly demonic activity going on this darkest of worlds where people work on the streets. But, we repeat, not everything should be attributed to demonic activity. In some situations, if not most, the problem will need to be resolved by sensitive prayer and patient loving of the person as she comes back to spiritual, mental and physical wholeness.

Some deliverance can happen in undramatic ways. For example, during worship, freedom can be found: someone who used to be consumed by hatred may now choose to love. God's methods are limitless. If you find the kind of manifestations occurring which are given above, you will need to expel the demon in the name of Jesus. The manifestation is a demonstration of rebellion against God. But God is still in control. The demon cannot and will not get the better of Him.

We tend to want formulas for ministry, patterns and recipes we can follow to have quick resolution of other people's problems as well as our own. There are no formulas. God does not work according to formulas. He deals with infinite mercy with each individual, knowing their needs, their deepest desires and their frailties and strengths. He gives signposts in His Word to help people to work out their salvation in fear and trembling.

The power is in Jesus' name. While we do not wish to give a formula, the sum and substance is 'get out and don't come back'. John Richards is particularly helpful here:

> 'A policeman who comes across a would-be intruder does not first retreat to his office and look up in his handbook what phrases to use authoritatively to drive him out. His authority does not lie in a formula but because he can speak in the name of the law. Whatever words he might use, they will convey the same message:*Get out, and don't come back.*' [2]

---

[2] Richards 1974, p. 164f.

But what happens after the demon has gone? In Luke 11:24–26, Jesus warns that it is possible for the demon to return and for the situation to become much worse than it was before the person was delivered. Here are some guidelines for follow-up care of those who have had deliverance ministry: [3]

- First, the person needs to accept that he or she can only be freed through Jesus Christ.

- Secondly, anything that is associated with or has been used in occultic practices such as books or objects should be destroyed.

- There should be confession and renunciation (in prayer) of all involvement with the occult [4]

- A prayer group should undertake to intercede for both the person and the person ministering to or counselling the girl.

- The person should have complete understanding of the nature of the forgiveness of sin through Jesus Christ.

- The person should continue to be supported by a prayer group and to be integrated into a community of believers where her faith will be built up and nurtured.

- The person should have no further contact *whatsoever* with people who are involved with the occult and/or spiritualism.

'The light shines in the darkness, but the darkness has not understood it.'
(John 1:5)

---

[3] These are adapted from a report produced by a working party on 'Spiritualism and the Occult' at the 1971 European Evangelism Congress in Amsterdam. They are reproduced in Richards (1974), p. 175.

[4] Neil T. Anderson's 'Seven Steps to Freedom' are particularly useful here.

Suggestions for further reading

Beattie, M. *Co-Dependent No More*. Center City, MN, USA: Hazelden, 1987.

Comiskey, A. *Pursuing Sexual Wholeness*. Eastbourne: Monarch, 1990.

Cossey, C. *My Story*. London: Faber & Faber, 1991.

Evangelical Alliance Policy Commission. *Transsexuality: A Report*. Carlisle: Paternoster, 2000.

Gaudry, E. *Recovery From Alcoholism: A Guide for Alcoholics and Those Who Help Them*. Victoria, Australia: Collins Dove, 1984.

Koch, K.E. *Christian Counselling and Occultism: The Counselling of the Psychically Disturbed and Those Oppressed through Involvement in Occultism*. Grand Rapids, MI, USA: Kregel Publications.

Little, P. *How to Give Away Your Faith*. Leicester: IVP, 1971.

McDonald, G. *Ordering Your Private World*. Guildford: Highland, 1984.

McMurran, M. *The Psychology of Addiction*. Bristol: Taylor Francis, 1994.

Minirth, F, Meier, P et al. *Beating Burnout: Balanced Living for Busy People*. New York, NY, USA: Inspirational Press, 1997.

Payne, L. *The Broken Image: Restoring Sexual Wholeness Through Healing Prayer*. Eastbourne: Kingsway, 1988.

Saia, R.M. *Counselling the Homosexual: A Compassionate and Biblical Guide for Pastors and Counsellors as well as Non-Professionals and Families*. Minneapolis, MN, USA: Bethany House, 1988.

Singlehurst, L. *Sowing, Reaping, Keeping: People Sensitive Evangelism*. Leicester: Crossway Books, 1995.

Yancey, P. *What's So Amazing About Grace?* Grand Rapids, MI, USA: Zondervan, 1997.

Notes

· ·
· ·
· ·
· ·
· ·
· ·
· ·
· ·
· ·
· ·
· ·
· ·
· ·
· ·
· ·
· ·
· ·
· ·
· ·
· ·
· ·
· ·
· ·
· ·
· ·
· ·
· ·
· ·
· ·

Notes

. . . .

. . . .

. . . .

. . . .

. . . .

. . . .

. . . .

. . . .

. . . .

. . . .

. . . .

. . . .

. . . .

. . . .

. . . .

. . . .

. . . .

. . . .

. . . .

. . . .

. . . .

. . . .

. . . .

. . . .

. . . .

. . . .

. . . .

. . . .

. . . .

. . . .

Notes

· ·

· ·

· ·

· ·

· ·

· ·

· ·

· ·

· ·

· ·

· ·

· ·

· ·

· ·

· ·

· ·

· ·

· ·

· ·

· ·

· ·

· ·

· ·

· ·

· ·

· ·

· ·

· ·

· ·

· ·

Notes

....
....
....
....
....
....
....
....
....
....
....
....
....
....
....
....
....
....
....
....
....
....
....
....
....
....
....
....
....
....
....

Notes

....
....
....
....
....
....
....
....
....
....
....
....
....
....
....
....
....
....
....
....
....
....
....
....
....
....
....
....
....
....
....

Notes

· ·

· ·

· ·

· ·

· ·

· ·

· ·

· ·

· ·

· ·

· ·

· ·

· ·

· ·

· ·

· ·

· ·

· ·

· ·

· ·

· ·

· ·

· ·

· ·

· ·

· ·

· ·

· ·

Notes

....
....
....
....
....
....
....
....
....
....
....
....
....
....
....
....
....
....
....
....
....
....
....
....
....
....
....
....
....
....

Notes

. . . .

. . . .

. . . .

. . . .

. . . .

. . . .

. . . .

. . . .

. . . .

. . . .

. . . .

. . . .

. . . .

. . . .

. . . .

. . . .

. . . .

. . . .

. . . .

. . . .

. . . .

. . . .

. . . .

. . . .

. . . .

. . . .

. . . .

. . . .

. . . .

. . . .

. . . .

Notes